ROMANCING THE CLOCK

Marvin Karlins, Ph.D
University of South Florida

Prentice Hall

Upper Saddle River, New Jersey
Columbus, Ohio

Library of Congress Cataloging-in-Publication Data
Karlins, Marvin.
    Romancing the clock / Marvin Karlins. — 2ed.
       p. cm. — (Job skills neteffect series)
    Includes bibliographical references and index.
    ISBN-13: 978-0-13-503733-1
    ISBN-10: 0-13-503733-6
     1. Time management.   I. Title.
HD69.T54K37 2009
640'.43--dc22

                     2008018195

Editor in Chief: Vernon Anthony
Acquisitions Editor: Gary Bauer
Editorial Assistant: Megan Heintz
Production Manager: Wanda Rockwell
Creative Director/Cover Designer: Jayne Conte
Cover Illustration/Photo: Getty Images, Inc.
Director of Marketing: David Gesell
Marketing Manager: Leigh Ann Sims
Marketing Assistant: Les Roberts

This book was set in Goudy font by Aptara® and was printed and bound by Bind-Rite/Command Web. The cover was printed by Bind-Rite/Command Web.

Pearson Education Ltd., London
Pearson Education Singapore Pte. Ltd.
Pearson Education Canada, Inc.
Pearson Education—Japan

Pearson Education Australia Pty. Limited
Pearson Education North Asia Ltd. , Hong Kong
Pearson Educación de Mexico, S.A. de C.V.
Pearson Education Malaysia Pte. Ltd.

Prentice Hall
is an imprint of

9 8 7 6 5 4 3 2 1
ISBN-13: 978-0-13-503733-1
ISBN-10:   0-13-503733-6

To the wonderful staff of Singapore Airlines.
Thanks for two decades of great memories!

Two Thoughts to Ponder

And in the end, it's not the years
in your life that count. It's the life in your years.

—*Abraham Lincoln*

It is good to learn to manage time . . .
but it is even better to manage
to have a good time.

—*Anonymous*

Contents

Preface   vii
About the Author   viii

What My Doctor's Appointment
Taught Me About Time Management   1

1   Don't Accumulate Possessions
    That Create More Hassle Than Joy   5

2   Money Is Time: Use It to Purchase
    Positives and Sell "Shoelaces"
    in Your Life   15

3   Prune Your Interpersonal
    Relationships   24

4   Give the Green Face Syndrome
    the Red Light   29

5 Don't Get Down on Your Luck   35

6 Choose a Career As If a Third of
Your Life Depended on It: It Does   43

7 Revel in the Journey or Skip the Trip!   57

8 Don't Always Put Off Until Tomorrow
What You Can Enjoy Today   62

9 Avoid the Pitfalls of Perfectionism   66

10 Pursue a Healthy Lifestyle:
It Enhances Joyful Living   71

11 When You Must Do Battle . . .
Pick Your Fights with Care   87

12 A Metaphor to Live By   98

Exercises and Applications   103
Index   135

Preface
Don't Watch the Clock . . . Romance It!

This book is about time and how you can use it to love the life you live. The twelve Action Steps described in the following chapters help you use your time to accentuate the positives and reduce the negatives in your life. By taking these Action Steps, you will learn that *effective* time management is measured not in terms of hours *saved*, but in terms of hours *spent* in joyful living.

Go ahead and Romance the Clock! There's never been a better moment to start loving your time on this Earth.

ACKNOWLEDGMENTS

Special thanks go to Kristin Cunningham, Susan George, Anita Rhodes, and Elizabeth Sugg of Prentice Hall for their efforts on my behalf.

I also want to express my appreciation for the valuable insights provided by the reviewers of this work:

Ron Kapper
Professor Emeritus, College of DuPage
Professional Trainer

Joyce W. Fields, Ph.D.
Columbia College

Monty Lynn
Abilene Christian University

Their input has strengthened the book.

Marvin Karlins, Ph.D.

About the Author

Marvin Karlins received his B.A. degree from the University of Minnesota (Phi Beta Kappa and *summa cum laude*) and his Ph.D. in Psychology from Princeton University. He is the author of 23 books and more than 200 articles published in professional, academic, and popular journals. In addition to his writing activities, Professor Karlins has been interviewed on radio and television talk shows worldwide and served as an international consultant to major companies, focusing his efforts in the aviation industry (where he consulted with Singapore Airlines for 20 years). Dr. Karlins is currently a Senior Full Professor of Management in the College of Business Administration at the University of South Florida.

Introduction
What My Doctor's Appointment Taught Me About Time Management

I don't know about you, but I look upon doctor's appointments as painful necessities—particularly those that involve being told that (a) you "might experience a slight discomfort" and/or (b) you are confronted by a person in possession of a latex glove and a tube of lubricating jelly.

Thus, I wasn't in a state of joyful anticipation when I scheduled my annual physical which, I knew, would include a prostate examination (a procedure where the doctor uses his finger to probe a small gland inconveniently tucked away in an orifice where the "sun doesn't shine"). The fact that the waiting room was full of patients when I arrived didn't lift my spirits; nor did the nurse who informed me the doctor was "running behind" (quaintly put) when I checked in at the front desk. After signing the traditional release form holding the physician blameless should any number of ugly medical consequences occur during my course of treatment, I was directed to take a seat and wait for my name to be called.

To pass the time I decided to check out some magazines on the table beside my chair. I selected one that specialized in self-help topics and began reading an article entitled "Time Management: How to Stretch Each Hour of the Day."

Bad decision!

Learning how to prolong time while undergoing a prostate examination was not my idea of a goal worth pursuing. In addition, the word *stretch* seemed particularly discomforting.

All of which got me thinking about the meaning of time management; thoughts which crystallized quickly when, at last, my name was called and I was led into the examination room where the doctor, latex glove in place, informed me that "You might experience a slight discomfort," and then assured me that ". . . this will only take a minute."

From a traditional time management perspective, the brief prostate portion of my physical was a success: It truly expanded my experience of available time. In fact, it was the longest minute of my life! If every minute passed that slowly I might well achieve subjective immortality. However, I quickly realized the difference between "quantity" time and "quality" time—and how one was pointless without the other.

Which brings me to the central thesis of this book: *Time management, as it is traditionally taught and practiced, fails to enrich our lives because it fails to consider this simple premise:*

What is important is not how much time you have but rather, how much you enjoy the time you're having.

What good is time management for people who are unhappy with the time they have? Does it help to use time more effectively to maximize unpleasant hours? Does the individual who hates work cry out for more time on the job?

Does the inmate who marks the passage of days by scratchmarks on the jailhouse wall seek ways to extend the hours between sunrise and sunset? Does the person in physical and/or mental agony await the start of daylight savings time so he or she can savor a 25-hour day?

Indeed, time management doesn't seem to be a major concern for people who are not enjoying their lives. If anything, these individuals speak of having "*too much* time on their hands" or needing to "kill time." Perhaps the most graphic example of this time management pathos is provided by a man from Illinois who claimed "The last thing I need in my life is more time" and promptly put a .45 caliber bullet through his brain.

Here is the simple truth:

If you're not enjoying your time you don't need to manage your hours, you need to manage your life!

And that's what this book is about: how to have *the time of your life*; how to take actions and make choices that will enhance the time you do have and make you want to savor your time rather than "kill" time.

The greatest tragedy in life, and the greatest waste of time, is to live—as Henry David Thoreau labeled it—a life of "quiet desperation . . ." a life full of hassles rather than happiness, a life that doesn't see the glass as half full or half empty but as half empty and full of germs! Perhaps the young man on his deathbed said it best of all:

"I'd rather spend 30 years loving life than 60 years just living it."

WHY SAVE TIME IF YOU DON'T SPEND IT WISELY?

All of us have a designated amount of time on this Earth. The question we should be asking ourselves is not how can we most effectively *use* that time but, rather, how can we most effectively *enjoy* it. I find no satisfaction or solace in the statements of those who speak of saving time while living lives in distress; that is *waste* management. The real value of time management can be measured by how well people have the *time* of their lives; how effectively they *manage to find time for joyful living*.

The premise of this book, then, is totally transparent: Learning to manage your time is worthless if you aren't enjoying the time you have! What you need to do is use your time to accentuate the positives and reduce the negatives in your life. How you can do this, of course, is the major theme of this book.

On the following pages I outline **12 Action Steps** you can take to get your life headed in a *positive* direction and make your time more *personally worthwhile*.

A DISTINCTION BETWEEN COMMON SENSE AND COMMON PRACTICE

As you read through the 12 Action Steps to a more enjoyable life you might think some of them are simply common sense notions. Perhaps some are. But let me assure you as a psychologist who has observed people's behavior for well over a quarter-century: *There is a vast difference between common sense and common practice when it comes to applying the 12 Action Steps to achieve more joyful living.* By this I mean that many more people claim to know these steps and use them than actually do. They talk a good game when it comes to practicing the 12 Steps in their own lives, but it's only "lip service." When it comes to actually *applying* the steps they fall far short of the mark; they simply don't "walk the walk" in their everyday behavior.

Don't let yourself be one of those people!

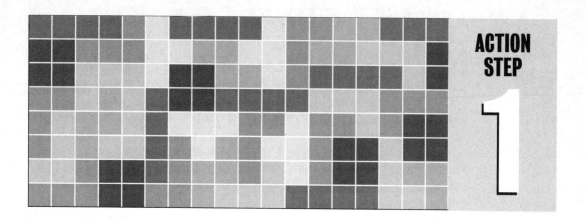

Don't Accumulate Possessions That Create More Hassle Than Joy

In our capitalist culture, which emphasizes the accumulation of wealth and canonizes the conspicuous consumer, our first Action Step borders on the heretical. After all, we have been nurtured and nourished on sound bites that remind us to "keep up with the Joneses," embrace the edict that "bigger is better," and seek "gratification NOW." To suggest otherwise sounds, well, downright un-American!

But if we're not careful we can end up paying a very high price indeed for our "possession obsession." That price becomes painfully obvious when we become slaves to what we own: when what we *have* creates more problems than solutions, more pressures than pleasures. I learned this first hand, as a teenager, when my father brought home . . .

5

A BOAT OVER TROUBLED WATER

I was 15 years old when my father decided to purchase a 26-foot cabin cruiser. It wasn't a decision lightly taken. Our family wasn't wealthy and such a purchase represented a significant financial liability. Add to that the fact that we lived in Minnesota, where the boating season, like the summer, was restricted to a few short months between snowstorms, and you had the potential for some serious problems.

Because my dad had spent so much money on the boat, and—because the weather offered him such limited opportunities to use it—he felt compelled to spend every usable weekend on the water to justify the price he paid for his recreational activity.

The man became a weather fanatic. His entire mood seemed to ebb and flow with the forecasts and the tides he so judiciously studied. A midweek prediction of weekend rain produced instant consternation; an actual "washout" on either Saturday or Sunday and my dad turned into a *very* unhappy parent—a condition I came to refer to as "boater's remorse."

It got to the point where each week of the sailing season was predicated on the need to get "fair usage" out of the boat: It was either sail or fail.

The boat had taken over my father's life. And ours.

Fortunately, my dad was neither a stubborn nor a foolish man. After two years of this "sea sickness" he realized that rather than his owning the boat, the boat had come to own him. Furthermore, his purchase was causing him more problems than pleasures—*more hassle than it was worth!* What had begun as the realization of a dream had turned into the recognition of a nightmare, so my dad sold the boat. He got the burden off his back. No longer did he worry and fret about the weather; no longer did he have to include the boat in every weekend plan; no longer did he have to give up other desired purchases to pay for the servicing and operation of the family vessel.

And you know the most amazing thing of all? Once he got out from under the boating burden he felt an instant sense of relief. He wondered aloud how he could ever have let such a thing cause him so much grief and unnecessary worry. He was amazed at how something he had wanted so badly had ended up hurting him so badly . . . and how long he had put up with it!

And do you want to know the other amazing thing? The day he sold that boat he *never looked back.*

WE ALL HAVE OUR "BOATS OF BURDEN"

What about you? Do you have possessions that create more hassle than joy? You probably do, and sometimes these possessions are more hassle than joy *not* because they overburden you financially, but because they make too great a demand on your time; they make you do things you'd rather not do. A pet is a perfect example of just such a possession.

THE LA(M)P DOG

Several years ago my daughter wanted me to get her a puppy. Knowing that puppies grow into dogs, and that dogs can be more of a hassle than a joy, I tried to get her to settle for a goldfish. Goldfish, after all, are inexpensive, easy to care for, don't last long, and can be used to teach children about death and dying.

She didn't buy it. Not only did she want a puppy, but she wanted a specific kind, a *shi-tzu*. Now, any dog that is called by that name should provide ample warning to any prospective buyer who might consider it a "first-choice" purchase. Further information reveals that the Chinese killed every one of these canines, except for eight that were smuggled out of the country, thus providing further evidence that this might not be the kind of dog you want in *your* home.

I was prepared to reject my daughter's request until she smiled at me and pointed to her hand, where daddy is wrapped around her little finger. Then she threw in the clincher: "Daddy, I'll take care of the dog," she promised. "You'll see." (A slight digression: Most children's conception of "taking care of a dog" would condemn the animal to a slow death. Therefore, if you're the adult in these circumstances, be prepared to assume some, if not all, dog-rearing and maintenance functions.)

We selected a *shi-tzu* puppy and brought it home. It turned out to be a disaster. At the possible risk of alienating all *shi-tzu* owners reading this book, I must tell you this animal quickly became more of a hassle than a joy. As it turns out, these particular dogs have an inherited characteristic that causes their eyelashes to grow inward toward their eyeballs, making the eyeballs itch and causing the dog to relieve the itch by rubbing its eye against any convenient surface (rug, grass, furniture). If left to rub its eye in such a manner, the dog will eventually lose its sight.

How do I know this? Because a dog ophthalmologist told me so. (Yes, Virginia, there are ophthalmologists for dogs.) Furthermore, the problem can be temporarily solved by paying the friendly veterinarian $800 to pluck out the offending hairs ("temporary" because the hairs can sometimes grow back, requiring another operation).

How do I know this? Because I paid such a fee. The only other choice, delicately put to our family as we learned of the diagnosis, was to "put the dog to sleep." When my daughter asked me what it meant "to put the dog to sleep," a young high school intern who was assisting the doctor answered by saying: "We kill it, honey."

My daughter decided in no uncertain terms that the "sleep" choice was *not* an option. So, operation completed, our pet was returned to us with a lampshade on its head. The lampshade was to protect the eye and keep the dog from reinfecting it by rubbing it on some foreign object, like the living room carpet. It also served to make the dog look like a furry lamp that would light up if you tugged its tail.

I successfully resisted the temptation to do this.

Sadly, our dog problems did not end with the operation. A few months later, lampshade freshly removed, the dog went outside and growled at a "walking stick," an insect that is capable of spitting an acid-like substance at its attacker. How did I discover this? Because the insect spit just such a substance into the *shi-tzu's* recently-healed eye—the result of which was a second, volume discount $350 operation and a new lampshade.

We finally gave the dog away. My wife still hasn't forgiven me, and my daughter agreed to the deal only after getting two new kitties in return.

Don't get me started on catbox problems.

What did I learn from all this? That boats and dogs are possessions that can be enjoyable and highly satisfying for *some* people, but hassles that make life uncomfortable if not downright miserable for others!

I also learned there are two ways to stay clear of possessions not worth the hassle. The best way, of course, is not to accumulate them in the first place. It is far easier to say "no" to a possession before you own it than after you've taken it home! The less preferred way is to "cut your losses" and divest yourself of any possession that is causing you more grief than joy. Either way:

The fewer possessions you have that cause you hassles, the more enjoyment and satisfaction you will experience in your everyday life.

HOW TO HASSLE-PROOF YOUR POSSESSIONS

Alice and Bill Black were a happily married couple who wanted to live the American Dream. That dream included the purchase of a home. Their problem was that they wanted to live the Dream a bit too lavishly. Instead of buying a nice, affordable three-bedroom "starter" home in a middle-class neighborhood, they decided to go for the five-bedroom, six-figure, executive homesite in the gated community—a house they could barely afford.

To meet the higher mortgage payments and property taxes their executive home required, the Blacks both had to work harder. For Alice it meant taking a second job, for Bill it meant working long stretches of overtime. The idea of starting a family was put on hold; there was no time for children with a steady flow of 12-hour workdays. Vacations, long weekends at the beach, intimate candlelight dinners—forget it! The Blacks couldn't afford the time or the money to indulge themselves in such luxuries. Even personal time together—so necessary for the cultivation and enrichment of a successful marriage—was sacrificed in the desperate struggle to keep one step ahead of foreclosure.

You can write your own ending to the Blacks' unfortunate, but all-too-common, story. Did they keep their home at the cost of losing their marriage? Did they lose their home and all the effort they expended in trying to save it? Did they keep their home and their marriage but sacrifice their health and/or happiness? Did they ignore each other's needs in a desperate attempt to maintain a mansion when they might have found much greater interpersonal harmony and joy in a humbler home?

What about you? Is there a little Alice or Bill lurking in your personal behavior? Have you ever looked at that new car or expensive home entertainment center and decided to *possess* it even though you knew the cost might outweigh the benefits of your acquisition? Even more dangerous: Have you ever acquired a possession impulsively—without even *thinking* about the possible hassles such an acquisition might produce?

If so, take these steps to increase the probability that the possessions you acquire will be more of a joy than a hassle.

1. Before taking ownership of any possession, do a cost/benefit analysis of the potential acquisition. Compare the positives versus the negatives such a possession will create in your life. Although you might not be able to anticipate *all* the costs and benefits that could result from the acquisition, the simple attempt to consider the issue will often put the possession in its proper perspective.

2. Ask yourself: "Am I willing to make the sacrifices necessary to acquire a possession I want?" "For how long?" "Might I be better off using my resources to acquire different possessions?" "Do I really *need* this possession?" "Is there a substitute possession I can acquire that will make less of a demand on my resources?"

3. Recognize that the more "major" a possession becomes—the more resources you will have to expend to acquire it—the greater is the need to carefully consider whether or not it is worth acquiring.

4. Try to avoid impulse purchases, particularly of "big ticket" items. You can take a more reasoned approach to acquisitions by adequately considering the matter.

5. Recognize that life is not static. Circumstances change. What once might have been a positive possession can turn into a negative one should your

financial or personal life undergo a significant modification. Such a change might require jettisoning certain possessions that are dragging you down or keeping you from getting back on your feet.

6. Nobody is right all the time. If you acquire something and then realize you made a mistake, don't be afraid to admit your error and maintain the status quo. Do what you must to divest yourself of the possession. It is better to cut your losses than plunge further into financial or psychological debt. Remember my dad and his boat. When he finally came to grips with his error and sold the vessel, that's when he experienced clear sailing!

WHEN POSSESSIONS BECOME ADDICTIONS

One of the quickest and surest ways to change a possession from a joy into a hassle is to turn it from an activity pursued with moderation into an addiction pursued with loss of control. The person who eats an occasional candy bar can find joy in consuming it, but this joy can evolve into a significant hassle if the person becomes a "chocoholic" and starts devouring unhealthy amounts of chocolate.

The same is true for *any* possession or activity that can become an addiction. It is true for the person who drinks, gambles, shops, exercises, surfs the web, even for the individual who spends time and money to enhance his or her physical appearance.

When excess replaces moderation in the way we choose to use our possessions, the risk of addiction is enhanced and the probability that the possession(s) in question will become more of a hassle than a joy is increased.

In its most virulent form, addiction can fool us into thinking that the way we use our possessions brings us joy when, in fact, just the opposite is true.

It is beyond the scope of this book to deal with the treatment of these types of addictive possession problems; however, I do want to present you with an example of destructive addictive behavior that I witnessed. I do so to illustrate how dangerous and powerful addictive behavior can be and how it can turn a joyful activity into a pathological nightmare. I hope that if you see yourself in this example, you will do whatever you must to eradicate the dangers of addiction in your own life. Remember:

Addiction is one personal possession
*you **never** **want** to have!*

LAS VEGAS ON $60,000 A DAY[1]

It was my second day in "Lost Wages, Nevada," and things weren't going my way. I was in a posh casino on the Strip, exhorting two plastic cubes to come up with the point-number five; they weren't listening. "Seven . . . line away, pay the don'ts," intoned the stickman, and a sure-fingered dealer whisked my chips off the green baize layout.

It was then that "Mr. C" made his appearance at the table. He was wearing an old pair of dirty pants and a denim work shirt and, as he edged up to the rail, he looked like an auto mechanic ready to shoot a little craps on his lunch break. He took some crumpled bills from his shirt pocket and called for 20 nickel ($5) chips. The stickman shoved six dice in his direction and announced: "New shooter coming out." I eyed the unkempt Mr. C and decided he looked as frayed as my bankroll. I took it as a sign and decided it was time to take a break.

A few hours later, I was walking past the casino when I heard the unmistakable clamor of dice players at a hot table. A winning table is a noisy table—and a crowded one. Players shout out bets and cheer the shooter, while spectators push and shove to catch a glimpse of the game. By the time I reached the scene, people were stacked three deep around the table, and I had to crane my neck just to see the action. It was a big game. Lots of black ($100) chips dotted the layout. The players were hunched over the table like hungry wolves over a freshly killed carcass; now, however, they were feasting on the casino's chips, frantically doled out by harried dealers as number after number kept showing on the dice.

And who was at the center of all the tumult? None other than the slovenly Mr. C. This time, however, I hardly noticed his attire; far more imposing was the tray full of black chips in front of him. It was hard to believe. There must have been $20,000 there!

I watched Mr. C play. He was a *desperado*—a gambler's term for a player who likes to bet fast and hard. When a good hand shows, a desperado can take the casino for a bundle. When the dice are cold—well, a desperado can lose fast, too.

The dice stayed hot. Mr. C ran out of rail space to store his chips, and he began stuffing the overflow into his two shirt pockets. As the dice kept passing, he began to bulge noticeably in the chest area, giving him the appearance of a female impersonator with a lumpy bra. It was really quite comical, but nobody was laughing, particularly not the pit boss, who realized that the padding represented about $10,000 worth of house money.

I observed the game a while more, until the dice started chopping and players drifted from the table. Mr. C showed no sign of quitting, and I

[1]This segment was taken from M. Karlins, *The Book Casino Managers Fear the Most!* (Gollehon Books, 1998).

wondered if he'd have the good sense to pull in his horns and take down a profit. I made a mental note to check back at the tables after taking in dinner and a show.

I saw Mr. C again five hours later. He was still at the same craps table, tossing black chips onto the layout from a stack he kept cupped in his right hand. His shirt pockets were still stuffed, and now there were significant bulges in his pants pockets as well. Mr. C was literally bloated with casino chips, and his gluttony was not going unnoticed. A security guard kept a knot of curious onlookers a respectable distance from the table, while several floorpersons and the shift boss watched the action from the dice pit.

I wondered about Mr. C's endurance—and his luck. Could either hold out much longer? I overheard a boxman tell a dealer that Mr. C had been going nonstop for over nine hours. All that action at high stakes can do funny things to a person's head. I took a closer look. Mr. C's movements had slowed a bit, and he was drinking steadily; still, he didn't look like a man about to call it a night. I remembered Einstein's observation about God playing dice with the universe and wondered if He had designated Mr. C to be the shooter.

***

Morning is always too early in Las Vegas. I woke up around 11:30 and decided a good deli lunch would shake yesterday's cobwebs from my mind. I was on my way to the restaurant when I spotted Mr. C standing next to his suitcase, just a few feet inside the hotel entrance. He was still wearing the same dirty clothes, but his face looked different. There was a strange look in his eyes. I wondered what had happened.

"You know him?"

The voice caught me by surprise. It was a hotel bellman who had helped me with my bags several times.

"Do you know him?" the bellman repeated.

"Not really. I saw him gambling yesterday," I answered.

"Did you hear what happened to him?"

"No, I was wondering about that."

The bellman shook his head. "He was winning a lot of money . . . "

"I know, must've been $40,000."

"More like 60. They had to send out the racks to get the chips to the cage."

"He cashed in?"

"Nope. Safekeeping. When he got to $60,000 he decided to take a break."

"To his room?"

"That's the real joke. He didn't *have* a room. He was a drifter, passing through."

"No job?"

He said he was a pipefitter from Chicago, going to L.A. to find work. He stopped off in Vegas as a lark."

"He must've had some money," I interjected, "I saw him buy in for a hundred at the tables."

"That was his *whole* bankroll, the last hundred bucks to his name."

"You sure?"

"Absolutely," the bellman replied. "He built a toothpick into a lumber-yard."

"That's pretty hard to believe," I said.

"If you think that's hard, listen to this!" The bellman waved his arms with a flourish. "When the shift boss found out the guy didn't have a room, they gave him a penthouse suite and sent him right up."

"One suitcase and all?" I asked wryly.

"That's not all they sent up there." The bellman gave me a wink.

"Looks like the management didn't want to see Mr. C abscond with his winnings."

"You got that right," the bellman agreed.

"Go on."

"Around eight o'clock the guy wakes up and staggers down to the casino. He's still got a hangover and he's walking bowlegged, but he remembers that money and he wants some heavy action. The swing shift was alerted and waiting for him—opened up a new table—the works."

"And he started betting fast and heavy . . . "

"He couldn't get it down fast enough. He was covering all the numbers and taking the field at a thousand a pop."

"I know—I watched him yesterday."

"Well, yesterday the dice were passing; this morning they weren't."

"Did anyone ever tell you you're quite a philosopher?" I said sarcasti-cally, looking first at the bellman and then at Mr. C still camped near the doorway. "How long did it take to break him?"

"About an hour. He ran through every cent he had. When he was tapped out, they got his bag from the suite, gave him some walking money, and told him to hit the road."

"Did he say anything to anybody?"

"What's there to say?" the bellman sighed, shrugging his shoulders. "The man lost $60,000 in an hour. That says it all."

***

In a way my bellman friend was right. What else *could* anyone say? An unemployed construction worker loses $60,000 in 60 minutes—certainly more money than he'll ever *make* in an hour. It's enough to scramble a per-son's brain. It must have scrambled mine, because suddenly I felt compelled to approach Mr. C and solicit his thoughts on the matter.

I walked over to where he was standing. "Excuse me," I said awkwardly, not knowing exactly how to begin. "Weren't you the guy I saw winning all that money at the tables yesterday?"

Mr. C turned and faced me directly. "Yes. But I lost it all back." There was no rancor in his voice, not even a hint of disappointment. He sounded matter-of-fact, like some person recounting a day at the office.

"*All* of it? You must have been winning thousands of dollars."

"All of it—$62,500 to be exact."

I couldn't understand how he could be so nonchalant. "My God, man! What happened? Why didn't you put some of it away?"

Mr. C stared at me with his strange blue eyes. They were wide and unmoving. "I wanted action."

Something about that response irritated me, and I snapped back: "Action? But for what? Now you have zero! You have nothing to show for it!"

My outburst didn't change Mr. C's composure, but it did elicit a response. "You're wrong," he countered. "I do have something to show for it."

"Oh, yeah? What?"

"*Memories.*" A wisp of a smile played across Mr. C's face. "I've got *memories* to show for it." And without another word, the unemployed pipe-fitter from Chicago picked up his suitcase, walked out the hotel door, and disappeared into the simmering heat of the Las Vegas afternoon.

***

Money. Boats. Pets. Houses: *All* possessions, all capable of bringing you a less stressful, more joyful life or a more hassled, unhappy existence.

The possessions you acquire and how you use them will go a long way in determining whether you end up with time *quantity* or time *quality* in your life. It is vital to establish the appropriate relationship between yourself and your possessions: *Always* own them, but *never* allow them to own you.

Don't accumulate possessions that create more of a hassle than a joy.

That's the first significant step you can take to *Romance the Clock* and live your hours joyfully. Let's turn now to Step 2.

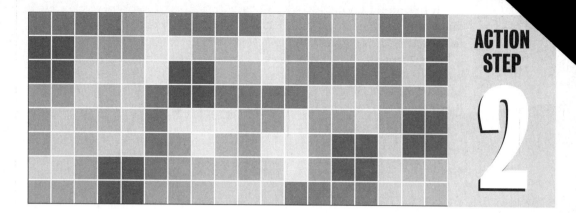

Money Is Time

Use It to Purchase Positives and Sell "Shoelaces" in Your Life

You've probably heard the saying "Time is money." This statement emphasizes the importance of money *over* time. It's a catchy phrase. The only problem is, it's *wrong!* When you consider the matter carefully, it turns out that *"money is time"* is the phrase of choice. Why? Because money is literally unlimited, we can amass far more than we could ever use; but time, on the other hand, is finite and precious. We can *never* seem to get enough of it; particularly *quality, joyful* time.

By emphasizing that money is time, Action Step 2 suggests that *we should use money to "buy" time—quality time—and we can do this by spending our disposable income on things that increase happiness and reduce hassles in our lives.*

Action Step 2 also suggests that possibly the most misguided, pitiful individual ever to walk the Earth is the multimillionaire who is hassled! Every time I encounter these individuals the first question I ask them is: "How can you be hassled when you can use your money to eliminate most of the negatives and accentuate the positives in your life?"

ey don't know the right answer, the second question I ask is: "How
ill you pay me to find out?" Just kidding! Actually, it's not difficult
how to use money to create quality time in your life. It just requires
digm shift" in your thinking, a willingness to change your old mind-
ut wealth and see money as time rather than the other way around—
aluable tool you can use to make your life more enjoyable and
free. It requires you to recognize that money *can* buy happiness and
reduce unhappiness, when it is used properly.

KEEP OFF THE GRASS: MY FIRST LESSON IN MONEY IS TIME

I don't know about you, but one thing I *hate* to do is mow the lawn, particularly in Florida, where mosquitoes are so large they need landing clearance
to alight on your arm and the grass grows faster than the national debt.
During the scorching summer months one can get sunstroke, poison ivy,
skin cancer, and dengue fever just getting the mower started! It's a thankless
job, plain and simple.

The problem is, my wife hates mowing the lawn, too, and she thinks it's
a *man's* responsibility to accomplish the task! In addition, my wife is *very*
persuasive, so for the first few years of our marriage I was the Laborer of the
Lawn, the Man on the Mower.

Each week was the same. From Monday through Friday I would dread
the weekend, knowing that Saturday or Sunday was reserved for mowing
the lawn. If I was lucky it would rain on Saturday ("Sorry, honey, it's light-
ning out there"), and I could postpone the task until Sunday, when, if I hit
the "daily double" and it rained again, I'd get a one week mowing reprieve.
Of course, that didn't normally happen, so I was stuck with no choice but to
do the dreadful deed. Between worrying about the mowing and actually
doing it, lawn care was becoming the bane of my existence!

Then one Tuesday it happened. I was looking out of my living room
window when I saw a white van pull up and park in the driveway next door.
A man got out and walked to the back of the van. Being a good citizen, I
walked outside to make sure no illegal act was about to be perpetrated on
my new neighbor, who had just moved in the week before.

It turned out that my concerns were unwarranted. In fact, the man was
quite the good Samaritan: he pulled a mower from the back of his van and
prepared to cut my neighbor's lawn!

I guess he must have noticed me watching him, because he walked over
and introduced himself as Ted, from Ted's Lawn Service. "I'll be mowing
your neighbor's grass," Ted explained. "Would you be interested in having
yours done?"

Now I'm not stupid. I was aware that lawn services existed but somehow, probably because of my upbringing, I always felt it was "cheating" to

use them. Like it was my *solemn duty* to cut the lawn. My moral responsibility. Something *civilized people did as a matter of course*, like saluting the flag and giving up one's seat to the elderly on a public bus.

But now I was being confronted by a man who *wanted* to cut the lawn *for* me. I hadn't asked him to do it—I wasn't *responsible* for his actions—he had *volunteered* to perform the odious task.

My heartbeat quickened. "How much?" I blurted out.

The man walked the perimeter of my yard.

I held my breath.

"A hundred bucks a month," he said finally, "edging included."

No gunslinger from the Old West could have whipped out his gun as quickly as I snapped out my hand to shake on the agreement.

This is not to say I closed the deal devoid of guilt. I still had this vague feeling of being irresponsible, a feeling that only lasted, I am glad to say, until the first time Ted mowed our lawn. Then I wondered why I had waited so long to get a lawn service in the first place!

I couldn't believe my good fortune: for $100 I was able to eliminate one of the greatest hassles in my life. No longer did I have to worry all week about cutting the grass and then actually *do* it. Now I could look forward to the weekend with joy rather than trepidation. Best of all, I was able to take the time I would have spent cutting the lawn and use it to do something I enjoyed—consulting—which ended up bringing in more income than the lawn service cost. So I actually *made* money in the process. And, of course, I was helping both the country's economy and Ted by giving him a job.

What a deal!

Now, please don't get me wrong! If you happen to be one of those "country squires" who finds pleasure in mounting your John Deere and trimming the lawn, then by all means, mow away. The last thing you'll want to do is spend your money to get the task done by someone else. But if you don't like the experience of lawn maintenance, and can afford it, I recommend you use your financial resources to enhance your quality of life—and do as the sign says, "Keep off the grass!"

CAN YOU AFFORD TO ADOPT ACTION STEP 2?

Let's be realistic. Most of us don't have unlimited wealth. Our financial resources are finite; thus, we must often make choices when it comes to getting the biggest "bang for our bucks."

For some of the readers of this book—particularly young people just getting started with families and/or careers and those on small, fixed incomes—freeing up enough money to take full advantage of this Action Step will be a challenge. Yet, it is amazing how many people with limited

incomes can still make use of some money to accentuate positives and reduce hassles in their lives. You don't have to be a millionaire to earmark
some funds for making Action Step 2 work for you. Even a few hundred
dollars, well spent, can make a significant difference in your life.

And don't forget this:

*Some of the money you use to save
time avoiding activities you don't like
to do can be recouped by using that
saved time to make money
at activities you do like to do.*

That's exactly what I did when I used the time I saved mowing the lawn
to make *more* money doing something I liked (consulting) than it cost me
to have the grass cut by a lawn service.

IF YOU DON'T HAVE THE BUCKS, CONSIDER BARTER

One other way (besides the use of money) to get out from under hassles and
into more pleasant activities is to recognize that "one man's meat is another
man's poison." In other words, what you might enjoy or at least not mind
doing could be repugnant to an acquaintance or friend. What this suggests
is the possibility of "trading off" various activities between individuals in
such a way that everyone involved ends up better off from the standpoint of
personal satisfaction and quality of life. If, for example, you don't mind
doing lawn work but hate driving the kids to and from school, and you have
a neighbor who detests mowing the grass but has no problems shuttling the
kids to their classes, you can barter services. Both parties to the agreement
can eliminate hassles *at no financial cost.*

As is the case when money is used to "buy" quality time and reduce hassles, it is amazing how many opportunities exist for bartering away negatives
and accentuating positives in your life. It does require some searching to
find people with needs that complement your own; but bartering is both a
reasonable and a workable approach to gaining positive time in your life
without actually spending money.

Whether you decide to use your bankroll, barter, or both to *Romance the
Clock*, it's important that you know . . .

HOW TO DETERMINE WHEN ACTION STEP 2 IS RIGHT FOR YOU.

Because most people aren't accustomed to a mindset that encourages the use of money to buy quality time and hassle reduction, they need guidelines to help them determine when such financial opportunities exist. Each of you will have to determine for yourself—based on your financial resources and particular likes and dislikes—when you should engage in Action Step 2. Here are four questions you should ask in arriving at your decision(s):

The four critical questions:

1. Whenever you are called upon to carry out some task or undertake some action, ask yourself: "Is this something I will enjoy doing?" If your answer is **"Yes,"** go forth and do it with a smile on your face! If, on the other hand, your answer is **"No,"** then ask yourself question 2:

2. "Can I pay someone to do the task or undertake the action for me?" If the answer is **"Yes,"** then answer question 3:

3. "Can I afford to pay the price they require?" If the answer is **"Yes"** again, then ask this final question:

4. "Will I gain enough benefits (e.g., increased quality time, decreased number of hassles) to justify paying the price required?"

   If your answers to questions 2, 3, and 4 are all affirmative, then I say: "Go for it!" I doubt that you'll ever regret your decision.

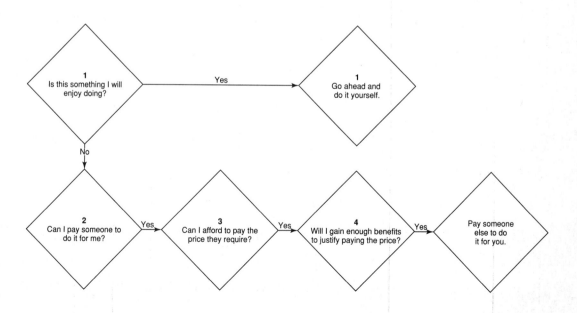

BUT ISN'T THIS A FORM OF BEHAVIOR ELITISM?

When I present Action Step 2 at seminars it is sometimes met with resistance by those who feel that spending money to get other people to do your dirty work is a form of elitism that is not in keeping with the democratic ideals of American society. I do not share their view in this matter. In fact, I would argue that the opportunity to use Action Step 2 is a natural outgrowth of our economic system at work. When you think about it, the basis of capitalism is differentiation between people: the ability of one person, through hard work, creativity, and/or luck (to name a few factors), to accumulate more than his or her neighbor. What makes capitalism work is the competition inherent in the system—the knowledge that people are *not* going to be treated equally when it comes to such things as financial rewards and benefits. This is what motivates people to work harder—the knowledge that success and the rewards that come with it are not equally distributed across all individuals.

If you have worked hard enough, or have been fortunate enough to accumulate money and wish to use some of it to increase the positives and reduce the negatives in your life, then you should do so without guilt. You'd be foolish not to: It's the capitalist way!

THE BROAD SPECTRUM REACH OF ACTION STEP 2

Once you are willing to use Action Step 2, I think you will be pleasantly surprised to discover how often it can be used to improve your quality of life.

To demonstrate this, take a piece of blank paper and write down all the unpleasant tasks you have to perform, tasks you would prefer *not* to do, if you had the choice. These can involve tasks at home and at work. Then see how many of these tasks can be reduced or eliminated by using money.

Also make a list of all the *positive things* you enjoy in your life; things you already do, would like to do, or would like to do more frequently. Again, these positive things can occur at home, at work, or both. Then ask yourself, "Is there any way that I can use money to enhance/increase/make possible these positive things I enjoy?"

Making lists that help you identify the positives and negatives in your life is an important part of using Step 2 most effectively. It doesn't take much time, and it often provides insights into your life that might be difficult to achieve in any other way.

If you have a close friend, partner, or spouse, it might also be beneficial to have that person make a list of what he or she thinks are the factors (experiences) you find positive and negative in your life. Sometimes others spot things you can't because they have the advantage of seeing you from a distance (a perspective you don't have because you're too close to the subject matter!).

MY "SHOESTRING" BUDGET

In examining the scientific literature on excessive stress and how it damages the human body, we discover that it's not only the major crises and traumas that get us, it's also the culmination of all the little annoyances, such as a broken shoelace.

I believe this. For that reason I earmark a large amount of my Action Step 2 budget to eliminate the "shoestring" hassles in my life. Once again, what is a hassle for me might not be a hassle for you; each of you must decide for yourself what annoys and hassles you—what your *breaking shoelaces* are. Then you can determine whether there is a way you can free up some finances to reduce or eliminate these problems in your life.

Because I suffer from a bad case of impatience, I am particularly hassled by events that slow me down or require me to do things that keep me from more important matters in my life. Therefore, my "shoestring" budget includes a lot of items that help me avoid these hassles whenever and wherever possible. Here are a few examples of expenditures I make to improve the quality of my life. (Please note that I couldn't afford many of these expenditures earlier in my life and that I added additional items only when my financial condition improved to a point where I could afford them without compromising my own or my family's basic quality of life.)

1. I pay others to do tasks I don't want to do myself. This includes lawn care, housekeeping, handyman jobs (e.g., clean gutters, paint house, pick up and haul trash not accepted by mainstream garbage collection service), auto cleaning, and tax return preparation, to name a few.

2. I pay for delivery services, even when I am charged a premium for the convenience. Such services include, but are not limited to, the delivery of restaurant food, dry cleaning, bottled water, groceries, mailed documents, and furniture. (When the furniture comes with "assembly instructions" I always pay the delivery people to assemble it, too!)

3. I will pay ticket agencies extra fees for seats to popular shows rather than spend hours calling or "camping out" for tickets that might be sold out by the time I get through to an operator or to the front of the line.

4. Sometimes government agencies and private businesses will allow you to "shortcut" time-consuming, unpleasant tasks (e.g., standing in line to renew licenses, filling out forms) by paying them an additional fee to do it for you, usually through the mail. I gladly take advantage of these offers.

5. I don't do comparison shopping except for the *largest ticket items*. It isn't worth the time and hassle. In fact, I always wonder about people who spend 15 or 20 minutes searching for a gas station that will save them a few cents on fuel when they use up their savings looking for the bargain in the first place!

6. I use valet parking and/or taxis when I know parking will be a problem.

7. I eat out frequently to save the hassles of food shopping, meal preparation, table setting, and kitchen cleanup.

8. On major purchases, I pay for warranties that guarantee me "no hassles" if things go wrong and I need to get the item fixed or replaced.

9. When my consulting and/or frequent flyer mileage allows me an upgrade to first class, I take it. This allows me to bypass long lines at check-in and provides me "priority" baggage handling, meaning my bags will be among the first to reach the luggage carousel at my destination.

10. I tip generously at establishments that give me better service and/or special treatment (e.g., prompt service and attention to personal requests).

11. I don't care how old or new an appliance or automobile is. I keep it until it becomes unreliable. Then, to avoid hassles with a lot of repairs and uncertainties, I get a new one.

12. I will always pay a premium if it helps me avoid hassles (e.g., reserved versus general admission seating; guaranteed room; confirmed appointment).

13. I will expend funds to join certain Internet sites that save me time by performing functions or providing services I would otherwise have to do myself.

14. I pay extra for a phone with an answering machine and caller ID. This saves a lot of time and hassle by allowing me to track calls I need to know about and avoid those that would waste my time and energy.

***

As my 14-point list indicates, there are many ways you can use money to keep shoelaces from breaking—to reduce unpleasant tasks or hassles in your life. Don't forget that money can be used to *enhance* the positives in your life, too. Whether you use your discretionary income to accentuate the positives or reduce the negatives in your life, you will be *enhancing the overall quality of your life. You will be Romancing the Clock: Taking Steps to Love Your Time on Earth!*

Let me end this presentation of Action Step 2 with a final example of how a little extra money went a long way in solving a pesky headache in my life. The fact that it took me a long time to use money to accomplish this objective speaks volumes about how we are conditioned to believe that "time is money" and not vice versa. I hope you can break away from that mindset as one major way to love your time on Earth.

A TICKET TO CONTENTMENT

My wife and I both teach in the same department at the university. Because we work at a commuter campus, parking is at a premium and faculty parking permits are expensive—more than $100 per year. Recently, the Parking Services Department decided to give faculty the choice of buying a parking sticker to paste on their bumper (the traditional method) or a hang-tag they could attach to their rearview mirror. This meant, for the first time, that my wife and I could buy just *one* hang-tag and share it. This was possible because we taught on different days and could switch the hang-tag between our two cars, an option that wasn't possible when only the paste-on stickers were available.

It sounded simple enough, and we'd be saving $100 in the process.

Well, it *wasn't* simple. It took only a week before we began to forget to move the hang-tag from one car to the other, which created a real hassle when the "tagless" teacher arrived at work. At that point the only choice was to park without the hang-tag and risk getting a $20 ticket, or drive to the visitors' booth to pick up a one-day parking pass—a time-consuming, out-of-the-way, major hassle.

This jostling for the hang-tag went on for two months before we realized that the $100 saving was costing us parking tickets, arguments, and a decidedly lower quality of life.

The solution? We purchased another hang-tag. It was one of the happier days of my life. And that happiness has stayed with me, now that the hassle of the wandering hang-tag is over.

***

It's amazing how little things such as an extra hang-tag and $100 dollars can bring about a noticeable improvement in your quality of life. Add up several of these little things and you've got a real opportunity to accentuate the positives and/or reduce the negatives in your life. Don't underestimate Action Step 2 as you strive toward having the time of *your* life!

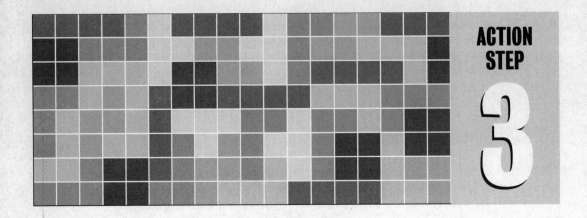

Prune Your Interpersonal Relationships

A few years back I heard an inspirational speaker tell a story I'll never forget. It involved a young man named Juan who had spent a lot of money to buy a new rug for his apartment. He was very proud of his purchase and went out of his way to keep it spotlessly clean.

One day a friend came to visit him. He carried a large plastic bag over his right shoulder. "I heard you got a new rug," he told Juan, "and I wanted to give you a special 'rug-warming' gift." With that, he opened the plastic sack he had been carrying and dumped about 20 pounds of rotting garbage onto the middle of the new carpet.

Needless to say, Juan was extremely unhappy with his so-called friend's behavior and threw him out of the apartment, telling him never to come back!

The motivational speaker paused for a moment to let everyone in the audience think about what poor Juan had just experienced. Then he finished the story.

"Here's what troubles me most," he exclaimed. "Whereas I'm sure each of you would toss out any so-called friend who dumped 20 pounds of physical garbage on your living room rug, the incredible thing is that a good many of you willingly put up with individuals who constantly dump heaps of mental garbage on you: insulting you, intimidating you, humiliating you, demeaning you—generally laying waste to your self-confidence and esteem."

The speaker left the audience to mull over his final question: "Why do we allow people to fill our heads with mental garbage and still associate with them, when we would recoil from individuals who fill our homes with physical garbage and banish them from our lives?"

Psychologists can suggest many reasons why people allow themselves to be "dumped on" by their "friends," accepting the hurt and self-destruction it creates. The reasons are interesting and varied, but they are not important from the perspective of this book. What is important—*supremely* important—is that you do not get embroiled in these kinds of sick interpersonal interactions at *any* level—acquaintance, friend, lover, associate, or spouse. To do otherwise is to risk unnecessary harm to your quality of life and psychological well-being.

PRUNE YOUR INTERPERSONAL RELATIONSHIPS

In agriculture, farmers keep their fruit trees in good shape by pruning them. This involves cutting away the deadwood and damaged sections of the tree that stunt its growth, thus allowing the healthy remaining portions to grow even stronger and more productive.

Each of us, like the farmer in the grove, needs to examine our interpersonal relationships and prune those that stunt our self-esteem, psychological health, and quality of life.

As the old saying goes, "There are millions of fish in the sea." Why surround yourself with people who are going to bring you down and make you feel less of a human being when you can choose to associate with those who will lift you up and enhance your view of yourself and your life?

You're not the city dump, so why let people treat you like one and dump all that mental garbage on you? And here's something else to consider: If you accept the mental garbage long enough, you might very well begin to believe you *are* the city dump.

THE LESSON OF THE "MIRACLE MAN"

One of the greatest inspirational films ever produced tells the story of *The Miracle Man*. It is a true story of a businessman/pilot who crashed his small plane and was almost given up for dead by the medical team assembled to treat him. The hero of the story realized that the only way he would ever recover from his accident was to ignore the pessimistic prognosis of his doctors and prove them wrong by his resolve and strength of will. Horribly injured, unable to walk, talk, breathe, even swallow on his own, the man literally willed himself to take small but significant steps on his memorable journey to recovery. At the end of the film he achieved something the medical community thought impossible: He walked out of the hospital under his own power!

As he got into a waiting automobile to go home, a nurse stepped forward to say good-bye. "You know what they call you at the hospital?" she asked, smiling at her newly discharged patient.

"No," he replied, a curious look on his face.

"The Miracle Man," she replied. And then she asked him about a little sign he had kept near his hospital bed, a sign with the word *SNIOP* written in capital letters. "I always wondered what those letters stood for," she admitted.

The "Miracle Man" smiled and told her the letters stood for being "*Susceptible to the Negative Influences of Other People.*" He told the nurse he stared at the sign to constantly remind himself that he had to mentally fight the negative beliefs and attitudes of the medical staff if he ever hoped to recover. He knew that once he started believing what *they* believed, then that belief would become a self-fulfilling prophecy and he would, in fact, end up exactly as the doctors thought he would: dead.

The "Miracle Man" then gave the small SNIOP sign to the nurse and told her to keep it, that "it might help somebody else, someday."

Well, that little sign can help you this day and every day thereafter. We are all, like the "Miracle Man," SNIOP: Susceptible to the Negative Influence of Other People. If we surround ourselves with people who treat us like garbage, then we will begin to think of ourselves as garbage; on the other hand, if we count in our circle of friends and loved ones people who treat us with respect and kindness, then we will begin to think of ourselves in positive terms and lead far more fulfilling, positive lives.

YOU ARE WHAT YOU EAT. YOU ARE WHO YOU ASSOCIATE WITH. GET YOURSELF ON A HEALTHY INTERPERSONAL DIET!

If you want a powerful tool for carving out quality time in your life—for accentuating the positives and reducing the negatives in your remaining years—then pruning your interpersonal relationships is a necessity. The sooner you get your "interpersonal house" in order, the sooner you can start enjoying the benefits of healthy person-to-person interaction and the enhanced quality of time that comes with it.

GET THOSE PEOPLE WHO ARE NEGATIVE INFLUENCES IN YOUR LIFE OUT OF YOUR LIFE!

Those "friends" who are negative rather than positive, discouraging rather than encouraging, who would rather criticize than compliment—*you don't need them!*

The spouse who "puts you down," who ridicules you and says you'll never amount to anything—*you don't need that kind of marriage partner!*

The associates who always point out your inadequacies and go out of their way to ignore your accomplishments—*you don't need those kinds of colleagues.*

Prune your interpersonal relationships!

Get rid of the deadwood in your life!

Separate yourself from those who would sap your strength and stunt your growth, and surround yourself with nurturing individuals who will help you fulfill yourself as a positive, joyous human being!

DON'T PRUNE YOUR RELATIONSHIPS WITHOUT DUE CONSIDERATION

Please don't misunderstand my intentions here. I'm *not* recommending you toss away your friends and/or spouse indiscriminately, at the first sign of a disagreement or conflict. Even the best of friends can have the worst of arguments! Good relationships take mutual effort to bloom. Like the gardener who wants his plants and trees to fully blossom you must nurture an interpersonal relationship with care, patience, and loving understanding if you want it to flower. The relationship can't be left to die at the first sign of blight. You need to be convinced that you've done as much as you can to save a relationship before you prune it away.

THE "HUMPTY DUMPTY" MOMENT

There is a time, however, when pruning becomes necessary to preserve your psychological health and quality of life. This time arrives *when you reach the point where you truly believe that no matter what you do—no matter how hard you try—the relationship between you and your significant other is irrevocably broken.* Implicit in this statement is the understanding that you have tried your best to make the relationship work.

I call this time the "Humpty-Dumpty moment" because, as you'll remember from the nursery rhyme, "all the king's horses and all the king's men, couldn't put Humpty Dumpty together again."

Humpty Dumpty was irrevocably broken, incapable of being fixed, permanently damaged beyond repair.

When *your* relationship with a person you care about reaches this point, when nothing you do or say can "put you back together again," then it's time to cut your losses and find a new friend on top of a different wall.

HOW DOES YOUR GARDEN GROW?

We might not always have total control over whom we interact with; for example, we might not be able to choose our colleagues at work. But when you do have a choice of companions, I hope you choose wisely, selecting individuals who have a positive influence on the amount of quality time you experience. "Trim away" those individuals who are a negative influence on you, who make you feel bad or stressed. They can create hassles you don't need in your life.

Look at it this way: In the world of people and plants there is poison ivy and there are perfumed roses. You can plant whatever you wish in your own personal garden—but never forget that you reap what you sow.

I hope you stop and plant the roses!

Give the Green Face Syndrome the Red Light

It was 1959–1960, a pivotal moment in America, a time of transition from the innocence of the fifties to the disillusionment of the sixties. I was in my first two years of undergraduate study at the University of Minnesota and an avid folk-guitarist, dividing my time between my academic assignments and my passion for folksinging. As part of my musical contribution I gave free folksinging and guitar lessons to students at the Hillel Foundation, a religious organization on campus. Anyone could attend the sessions, which included both group and individual instruction.

One particular session stands out in my mind. I was in the room reserved for my lessons, strumming a song on my guitar, when a young man appeared in the open doorway. I had never seen him before. I nodded "hello" and invited him in.

"I heard the guitar," he said, walking in and stopping a few feet from where I sat. "I play, too. Would you like to see?"

"Sure," I said, and handed him my guitar. He fingered a few basic chords and sang part of a "top 40" song. I could tell he didn't know much about the guitar *or* singing, but he did seem interested in what he was doing. For an instructor, interest is what makes teaching worthwhile.

The young man handed me back my guitar. "What kind of music was that you were playing?" he inquired.

"Folk guitar," I answered. "If you're interested, I give lessons for free."

"Really?" That seemed to catch my visitor's full attention. "When?"

"Every Wednesday at 2 P.M.—and other times if it's more convenient for you."

"OK—I think I'll stop by."

"Fine." I wondered silently whether he would actually return. "By the way, my name's Marv," I said, extending my hand.

"I'm Bob," he replied, and we shook hands.

As it happened, Bob did return. He was one of my "regulars." I always looked forward to the guitar lessons because they allowed me to do the two things I loved best: teaching and folksinging. And that's exactly what made things so difficult when, trying to balance my school obligations with my folksinging interests, I realized I couldn't pursue both activities and do justice to either. I reluctantly came to the conclusion that I would have to choose between a career in folksinging or one in academics.

I chose academics.

A few days after I announced the end of the folksinging lessons, I was approached by Bob. He wanted to know where he could continue to develop his folksinging skills now that I was no longer available as a teacher.

I thought about his request. In the short time he had been my student it had become obvious to me that Bob didn't have a gifted voice or a great command of the guitar; yet, if he was motivated enough to want to pursue folk guitar, who was I to object? "Try the 10 O'clock Scholar," I suggested. "It's a coffee house a few blocks from the campus, and there are always a few folksingers playing there."

He thanked me for the suggestion and went on his way.

It was the last time I saw Bob in person.

It wasn't the last time I would cross paths with him, however, although I didn't know it then.

Years passed. It was the fall of 1963. I was in my first year of graduate school at Princeton University, studying for my Ph.D. in psychology. Obtaining the degree required, among other things, a reading knowledge of two foreign languages. I chose French and German. The French was relatively easy; the German, on the other hand, was extremely difficult, with a grammatical structure totally different from English. I remember spending an entire month memorizing the principles in a book called *The Key to German Translation*, just so I could pass the language requirement and get on with my studies.

It was during the final week of this German review that it happened. I had decided to take a walk through the town of Princeton to unwind and get a breath of fresh autumn air. Princeton is a university town with many wealthy homes and (at that time) one major performing arts center called the McCarter Theater. As I strolled past the building, I noted the lighted marquee out front announcing the major coming attraction for the week-end. The illuminated letters spelling out the performer's name were large enough to read from across the street.

I knew who the performer was—although he had changed his surname since he had first asked me to teach him folk guitar. In those days his name was Bob Zimmerman. But now the sign read BOB DYLAN.

Seeing Dylan's name in lights at that particular moment was one of the worst experiences of my life. Here I was, a struggling student, spending an entire month trying to pass a German exam just so I could get through my first year of graduate school, and what do I see but one of *my* students who didn't sing or play guitar any better than I did, already achieving star status.

Of course, the fact that "my" student Bob had writing talents I never even dreamed of did not cross my mind at that moment!

Instead, I was totally immersed in a full-blown case of *The Green Face Syndrome*, commonly known as *jealousy*. "Why am I here and why is he there?" I mumbled, and railed against the unfairness of an unjust world!

It would be two decades before I could actually listen to a Bob Dylan song without going into a spasm of self-pity or jealousy. And I don't even want to *think* of how much time I wasted lamenting my misfortune in comparison to his good fortune.

Yet, in the end, Bob Dylan was a blessing of sorts for me. And he will be for you, too, if you learn in a few moments what it took me more than 20 years to discover: Jealousy—the Green Face Syndrome—is one of the most destructive forces in human existence. It makes life miserable, elevates pettiness, reduces quality time and self-worth, and leaves one angry and bitter. It is like a cancer spreading havoc over your psychological nervous system.

It's bad news!

Give the Green Face Syndrome a red light!

When I finally came to terms with my own jealousy and realized that my anger at Bob Dylan's success was both foolish and petty; when I could *accept* his fame without rancor and self-pity; when I stopped comparing his success with mine—I was able to eliminate the outflow of negative energy jealousy requires and transform that energy into a positive force for positive living.

WHY I TELL THE BOB DYLAN STORY

It took my encounter with Bob Dylan to make me realize the destructive power of the "Green Face Syndrome."

You simply cannot Romance the Clock when your time is consumed with jealousy.

The reason I tell the story is because of the widespread incidence of jealousy in our contemporary society. The Green Face Syndrome is a big problem, and I hope that when you read about the problems it caused me it will help you steer clear of it in your own life.

This Green Face Syndrome seems to be most pronounced when: (a) people we perceive to be no better than ourselves enjoy more success than we do; (b) we must confront these individuals directly or indirectly in our everyday life; and/or (c) these individuals tend to flaunt what they have, thus making it harder for us to ignore their achievements. Of course, there is also the more common "garden variety" of this syndrome: It occurs *whenever* we begin to think in terms of "The grass is greener on the other side of the fence." It seems that in our competitive, keep-up-with-the-neighbors society, very few, if *any* of us, can avoid being jealous at some point in our lives. My only hope in writing this chapter is to enlighten each of you to the dangers of this affliction and encourage you to reduce its prevalence in your behavior.

WHAT ABOUT YOU?

Be honest with yourself. Do you harbor jealousy toward others? Do you have the Green Face Syndrome toward your sibling(s)? Your spouse? Your friend? Your parents? Your associate at work? A neighbor who has more than you do? Some person you read about in the newspaper or saw on TV? If you do . . . don't feel alone. Envy, jealousy, the Green Face Syndrome by any name is a common human failing.

But that's *exactly* what it is: a failing.

If we can learn to save our energy for becoming all we are capable of becoming rather than squander it in anger or frustration over what someone else has become—we shall have the greatest chance to love all the years of our lives.

THE STORY OF THE DOG AND THE BONE

In many ways, the Green Face Syndrome brings to mind the fable of the dog and the bone. It seems that the dog in this particular story was very lucky: He had just found a juicy steak bone in an overturned garbage can and was on his way to a secluded spot to consume his prize. He trotted into an open field that was bounded on one side by a deep pool of water. As he moved past the pond something caught his eye and he stopped for a moment to gaze into the water. There, staring back at him, was *another dog with a bone in it's mouth!*

"Well," thought the dog, "two bones are better than one," and he momentarily dropped his prize so he could seize the other dog's bone. This was *not* a good idea. What the dog was seeing was his own reflection, and once he dropped his bone it fell into the water and sank out of reach.

The dog ended up with no bone at all.

The Green Face Syndrome occurs when we *reflect* on those around us and covet what they have. Like the dog, we aren't satisfied with our own good fortune, and in our longing to possess what others have, we risk losing the joy and satisfaction of possessing what is already ours.

We end up, like the dog, with a sad reflection of ourselves.

***

Don't waste your energy in jealous thoughts and actions. Put your energy where it can pay dividends: achieving your own goals and objectives. Forget about the success of others. What you succeed in doing for yourself and your loved ones will be the factor of enduring importance in your life.

A FINAL BIT OF IRONY

When I look back on my Bob Dylan experience with the advantage of hindsight and hard-earned wisdom, I realize that part of my jealousy stemmed from Bob's success at becoming what I wanted to be: a famous folksinger. The fact that I had given up any chance of achieving that fame when I chose academics over music didn't comfort me. It was almost as if Dylan's success made me believe I had made the wrong decision—that if only I had stayed with folk guitar I, too, could have had money, fame, and what many people want most of all: immortality, the feeling that they will live on forever through their works.

As I indicated earlier, that unhappiness cost me a great deal in terms of achieving quality time in my life. When I finally came to grips with who Bob Dylan was and who I was, and that it was okay for me to be me and not feel "cheated" by it—only then could I truly love the years I was living.

I must admit, however, that an event that occurred a few years after I had made peace with myself did a lot to put the need for "immortality" in proper perspective.

It happened during one of my classroom lectures in 1998. There, in front of 300 students, I was presenting the Green Face Syndrome and using my experience with Bob Dylan to highlight the negative consequences of jealousy. Upon completing my presentation I asked if there were any questions.

A student raised his hand. "One question," he said. "Who is Bob Dylan?"

***

The Green Face Syndrome is a major enemy of quality time in *anyone's* life. Don't worry about how others are doing, focus on yourself. Expend your energy on achieving your own objectives rather than tracking the accomplishments of others. And—oh yes—don't worry about gaining immortality through your works. Fame is fleeting. Be satisfied when, at the end of each day, you can say you achieved quality time in your life.

Don't Get Down On Your Luck

Sue Zera has an interesting story to tell. It's true, too. Seems that Sue worked as a tavern employee in Columbia, Illinois, where, as part of her duties, she sold lottery tickets to interested customers. On the day before the drawing she was busily punching up player requests into the lotto terminal when she hit the wrong key and the machine spewed out 50 incorrect tickets.

What to do?

Sue had no desire to purchase them. Unfortunately, nobody else did either. So she was forced to plunk down $50 of her own money to buy the unwanted tickets.

One can only assume that Sue Zera was one unhappy lady when she went home from work that night.

Well, the anger didn't last long.

The next day Sue Zera discovered that one of the tickets she had been forced to buy had just won her 10 MILLION DOLLARS!

***

Now I ask you: "Was Sue Zera lucky, or what?" Consider: The lady makes an error, doesn't want to buy the compromised tickets, is forced to make the purchase against her will, and ends up winning millions!

I mean, is that fair or what? Probably not.

But to paraphrase an old saying, "Luck happens."

Which is fine when it happens to you, but not so fine when it happens to someone else, particularly if that someone else ends up getting ahead of you because of a lucky break. That can result in an instant, severe case of the Green Face Syndrome, and cause you to gnash your teeth into pulverized stubs of their former selves.

Consider, for example, a wonderful essay entitled *Luck*, by master author Mark Twain. As you read the story imagine how you would feel if someone at your place of work were to outshine you, not because of talent or skill but, by incredible good fortune.

LUCK

It was at a banquet in London in honor of one of the two or three conspicuously illustrious English military names of this generation. For reasons which will presently appear, I will withhold his real name and titles and call him Lieutenant-General Lord Arthur Scoresby, Y.C., K.C.B., etc., etc., etc. What a fascination there is in a renowned name! There sat the man, in actual flesh, whom I had heard of so many thousands of times since that day, thirty years before, when his name shot suddenly to the zenith from a Crimean battlefield, to remain forever celebrated. It was food and drink to me to look, and look, and look at that demigod; scanning, searching, noting: the quietness, the reserve, the noble gravity of his countenance; the simple honesty that expressed itself all over him; the sweet unconscious of his greatness—unconsciousness of the hundreds of admiring eyes fastened upon him, unconsciousness of the deep, loving, sincere worship welling out of the breasts of those people and flowing toward him.

The clergyman at my left was an old acquaintance of mine—clergyman now, but had spent the first half of his life in the camp and field and as an instructor in the military school at Woolwich. Just at the moment I have been talking about a veiled and singular light glimmered in his eyes and he leaned down and muttered confidently to me—indicating the hero of the banquet with a gesture:

"Privately—he's an absolute fool."

This verdict was a great surprise to me. If its subject had been Napoleon, or Socrates, or Solomon, my astonishment could not have been greater. Two things I was well aware of: that the Reverend was a man of strict veracity and that his judgment of men was good. Therefore I knew, beyond doubt or question, that the world was mistaken about this hero: he *was* a fool. So I meant to find out, at a convenient moment, how the Reverend, all solitary and alone, had discovered the secret.

Some days later the opportunity came, and this is what the Reverend told me:

About forty years ago I was an instructor in the military academy at Woolwich. I was present in one of the sections when young Scoresby underwent his preliminary examination. I was touched to the quick with pity, for the rest of the class answered up brightly and handsomely, while he—why, dear me, he didn't know anything, so to speak. He was evidently good, and sweet, and lovable, and guileless; and so it was exceedingly painful to see him stand there, as serene as a graven image, and deliver himself of answers which were verily miraculous for stupidity and ignorance. All the compassion in me was aroused in his behalf. I said to myself, when he comes to be examined again he will be flung over, of course; so it will be simply a harmless act of charity to ease his fall as much as I can. I took him aside and found that he knew a little of Caesar's history; and as he didn't know anything else, I went to work and drilled him like a galley-slave on a certain line of stock questions concerning Caesar which I knew would be used. If you'll believe me, he went through with flying colors on examination day! He went through on that purely superficial "cram," and got compliments too, while others, who knew a thousand times more than he, got plucked. By some strangely lucky accident—an accident not likely to happen twice in a century—he was asked no question outside the narrow limits of his drill.

It was stupefying. Well, all through his course I stood by him with something of the sentiment which a mother feels for a crippled child; and he always saved himself, just by miracle apparently.

Now, of course, the thing that would expose him and kill him at last was mathematics. I resolved to make his death as easy as I could; so I drilled him and crammed him, and crammed him and drilled him, just on the line of questions which the examiners would be most likely to use, and then launched him on his fate. Well, sir, try to conceive of the result: to my consternation, he took the first prize! And with it he got a perfect ovation in the way of compliments.

Sleep? There was no more sleep for me for a week. My conscience tortured me through day and night. What I had done I had done purely through charity, and only to ease the poor youth's fall. I never had dreamed of any such preposterous results as the thing that had happened. I felt as guilty and miserable as Frankenstein. Here was a wooden-head whom I had put in the way of glittering promotions and prodigious responsibilities, and but one thing could happen: he and his responsibilities would all go to ruin at the first opportunity.

The Crimean War had just broken out. Of course there had to be a war, I said to myself. We could have peace and give this donkey a chance to die before he is found out. I waited for the earthquake. It came. And it made me reel when it did come. He was actually gazetted to a captaincy in a marching regiment! Better men grow old and gray in the service before they climb to a sublimity like that. And who could ever have foreseen that they would go and put such a load of responsibility on such green and inadequate shoulders? I could just barely have stood it if they had made him a cornet; but a captain—think of it! I thought my hair would turn white.

Consider what I did—I who so loved repose and inaction. I said to myself, I am responsible to the country for this, and I must go along with him and protect the country against him as far as I can. So I took my poor little capital and went with a sigh and bought a cornetcy in his regiment, and away we went to the field.

And there—oh, dear, it was awful. Blunders?—why, he never did anything *but* blunder. But, you see, nobody was in the fellow's secret. Everybody had him focused wrong, and necessarily misinterpreted his performance every time. Consequently they took his idiotic blunders for inspirations of genius. They did, honestly! His mildest blunders were enough to make a man in his right mind cry; and they did make me cry—and rage and rave, too, privately. And the thing that kept me always in a sweat of apprehension was the fact that every fresh blunder he made always increased the luster of his reputation! I kept saying to myself, he'll get so high that when discovery does finally come it will be like the sun falling out of the sky.

He went right along up, from grade to grade, over the dead bodies of his superiors, until at last, in the hottest moment of [a major battle] down went our colonel, and my heart jumped into my mouth, for Scoresby was next in rank! Now for it, said I; we'll land in Shool in ten minutes, sure.

The battle was awfully hot; the allies were steadily giving way all over the field. Our regiment occupied a position that was vital; a blunder now must be destruction. At this crucial moment, what does this immortal fool do but detach the regiment from its place and order a charge over a neighboring hill where there wasn't a suggestion of an enemy! "There you go!" I said to myself; "this *is* the end at last."

And away we did go, and were over the shoulder of the hill before the insane movement could be discovered and stopped. And what did we find? An entire and unsuspected Russian army in reserve! And what happened? Were we eaten up? That is necessarily what would have happened in ninety-nine cases out of a hundred. But no; those Russians argued that no single regiment would have come browsing around there at such a time. It must be the entire English army, and that the sly Russian game was detected and blocked; so they turned tail, and away they went, pell-mell, over the hill and down into the field, in wild confusion, and we after them; they themselves broke the solid Russian center in the field, and tore through, and in no time there was the most tremendous rout you ever saw, and the defeat of the allies was turned into a sweeping and splendid victory! Marshal Canrobert looked on, dizzy with astonishment, admiration, and delight; and sent right off for

Scoresby, and hugged him, and decorated him on the field in presence of all the armies!

And what was Scoresby's blunder that time? Merely the mistaking his right hand for his left—that was all. An order had come to him to fall back and support our right; and instead, he fell *forward* and went over the hill to the left. But the name he won that day as a marvelous military genius filled the world with his glory, and that glory will never fade while history books last.

He is just as good and sweet and lovable and unpretending as a man can be, but he doesn't know enough to come in when it rains. Now that is absolutely true. He is the supremest ass in the universe; and until half an hour ago nobody knew it but himself and me. He has been pursued, day by day and year by year, by a most phenomenal and astonishing luckiness. He has been a shining soldier in all our wars for a generation; he has littered his whole military life with blunders, and yet has never committed one that didn't make him a knight or a baronet or a lord or something. Look at his breast; why, he is just clothed in domestic and foreign decorations. Well, sir, every one of them is the record of some shouting stupidity or other; and, taken together, they are proof that the very best thing in all this world that can befall a man is to be born lucky. I say again, as I said at the banquet, Scoresby's an absolute fool.

LEARNING TO HANDLE LUCK IN YOUR LIFE

The Reverend in Mark Twain's essay suggests that "the very best thing in all this world that can befall a man is to be born lucky."

Is the Reverend correct? Can a person be born lucky? At this juncture in time there is no way to know. Science has no definitive answer.

But we do know that Scoresby was lucky.

So was Sue Zera with her 10-million-dollar lottery win.

In fact, the common lesson to be learned from Sue Zera's experience and Mark Twain's essay is that luck *does* play a role, in varying degrees, in *everyone's* life. We are all affected by it.

What is important is not whether luck happens (it does!) but how we respond to luck when it impacts our life.

From the standpoint of *Romancing the Clock*, the way we respond to luck will sometimes have more impact than the luck itself!

Having the right attitudes about luck can go a long way toward enhancing the quality of time in your life and reducing the hassles and frustrations that make a positive outlook difficult, if not impossible, to attain. What are the right attitudes when it comes to the "luck factor" in *your* life?

The Right Attitudes

1. *Luck is an inevitable part of life.* Be stoic in this regard. "Luck happens." But that's not all bad! Why not put a positive "spin" on luck—imagine how boring life would be without it! After all, luck makes our time on this planet more interesting by (a) making life more unpredictable and (b) leveling the playing field (allowing some people with lesser talent to prevail over those with inherently greater promise).

2. *Luck, by its very definition, is random and beyond our control. Don't waste time fretting over yours if it isn't all that great!* Hey, if you get dealt a bad hand in life, why make matters worse by dwelling on it or using it as an excuse to feel miserable and hassled? You had no role in *causing* the misfortune—why blame yourself and *act* as if you did? The best way to treat bad luck is to get over it and get on with your life.

   Remember: Luck *does* play a role in people's lives. We need to accept good fortune with gratitude and learn to roll with the punches when misfortune comes our way, picking ourselves off the canvas and hoping for a better outcome as we try again.

3. *We will experience both good and bad luck in our lives.* I emphasize this point because of our natural human tendency to interpret events as we want to see them. For instance, if we get a lucky break that moves us ahead in our job or personal life, the temptation is to view the success as something we earned or deserved. On the other hand, if we are the victims of misfortune that leads to a negative result in life and/or work, we immediately label it as "bad luck" and bemoan our fate.

   Also, a large percentage of people tend to remember what they want to remember and forget what they want to forget. If you happen to be a bit of a pessimist (and I think the majority of the world's population falls into this category!) then you will vividly recall when bad luck has befallen you but conveniently forget the times that luck has been on your side.

   I had a student who suffered from this "good luck/bad luck" memory problem. She came to me after she had missed a grade of "B" by one point in my course (she received a "C"). Of course, she attributed this to "bad luck"—after all, there were 180 points in the class and to miss by just one tiny digit was the worst kind of misfortune.

I asked this student whether she had ever *achieved* a higher grade by one point.

"No, I haven't," she replied. Yet, when I actually reviewed her other course grades with her we were able to identify *two* occasions when she had earned the next higher grade in the course (from a "C" to a "B" and a "B" to an "A") by one point.

It is understandable that you might complain when bad luck hangs over you like a heavy, dark cloud. Just don't forget the times that good luck has its innings and shines upon you like a bright sun on a warm summer day.

4. *Sometimes bad luck is a Prerequisite to good luck!* Think about it: I'm sure you can recall at least one personal experience when some misfortune or bad luck served as the impetus for improving your overall quality of life.

Thus, when bad luck appears in your life, don't despair! Remember that even *misfortune* can be the material from which *good fortune* can be fashioned. Remember that it takes rain to make a rainbow; lemons to create lemonade.

You can bet that Sue Zera understands how bad luck can be a prerequisite to good luck. Ten million dollars can help you understand the situation real quickly! Steve Johnston understands it, too. He couldn't believe his misfortune when a traffic jam made him miss his flight to a critically important business meeting. Later that day, still fuming over the missed meeting, Steve learned that the flight he was supposed to be on had crashed. Everyone on board lost their lives.

Sometimes bad luck today can be good luck tomorrow; sometimes misfortune tomorrow can be the force that guides us toward good fortune in the months and years to come.

I know some positive-thinking individuals who believe that bad luck is simply a doorway you must go through to find an unexpected opportunity. I like that kind of thinking! If you approach bad luck with such an attitude it won't guarantee you positive results, but it can elevate your spirit—and it *will* encourage you to look for that doorway!

DON'T PUSH YOUR LUCK!

At home. At work. At play. Awake or asleep. Luck is always out there, waiting to affect any and all aspects of our life. At times it appears that good luck avoids us like the plague while bestowing ample good fortune on those around us. At times we might wonder whether there is some grand conspiracy to ensure us misfortune at every turn.

Do not despair! Remember that even bad luck can be a tool from which good luck can be fashioned. And remember, also, that luck is unpredictable: a long era of good luck could be just around the corner.

But most important of all: Don't PUSH your luck. We "push" our luck when we let it negatively affect the way we feel about ourselves and/or others. We "push" it in the sense that we make it worse through such actions. Any type of luck becomes *unlucky* (and unhealthy) when we let it have a negative impact on the way we feel about ourselves, our time, and those around us.

Accentuating the positives and reducing the negatives in your life involves dealing with luck—good or bad—in a healthy, rational manner. It means making the most of good fortune when it comes your way and getting on with your life when misfortune befalls you. The next time you are experiencing difficult times in your own life, take heart from the words of a man who turned misfortune (lost his job in a corporate downsizing) into good fortune (in both senses of the word: He founded his own company and made millions!). His insight for us all:

**I cannot control my luck, but I can
control the way I respond to it.**

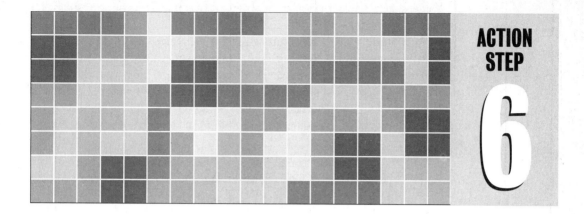

ACTION
STEP

6

Choose a Career As If a Third of Your Life Depended on It

It Does

> **Note:** If you are happy with your worklife (your job/career/profession) you can skip this section and go directly to Action Step 7.

Join me, if you would, in a journey of the imagination. I want you to pretend that you wake up one morning, get ready to leave your residence and . . .

Can't.

The front door won't open.

No matter how hard you try, it won't budge.

You test the back door and all the windows with the same result: You can't get out!

As you stand there, contemplating the weirdness of your situation, a person you have never seen before suddenly appears in the room before you.

"I suppose you're wondering why you can't get out the door," the stranger says.

"Who are you?" you reply.

"I'm a genie," the stranger explains, "and I'm here to see if you'll accept my offer."

You view the stranger skeptically. "I thought genies wore turbans," you argue. "And besides, genies grant wishes; they don't make offers."

"This is not turban weather," the stranger responds, pointing to the hot Florida sun filtering through the living room window. "Besides, this particular journey of imagination calls for an offer, not a wish."

You decide to go along with the stranger because you agreed to "pretend" at the outset of the chapter. Besides, you can't get out the door.

"Let's hear the offer."

The stranger nods his approval. "Here's the deal. If you're willing to remain in your residence—without leaving it even once—I will provide you with all the creature comforts you could ever want: new furniture, complete entertainment system, state-of-the-art kitchen appliances, computers, the works. I'll also supply you with all the food and drink you can consume. Just tell me what you want and you'll get it. Furthermore, I'll pay all your bills and costs. You don't have to pay a cent! All you have to do is stay here and not leave."

"Whoa! Wait a minute," you exclaim. "How could you do this?"

The stranger smiles. "Hey, this is a journey of imagination, remember? Well just *imagine* it can be done!"

"All right, fair enough," you agree. "So you're saying that you'll supply me with anything I want—food, drink, household furnishings, money to pay my bills—if I don't leave the premises?"

"That's right," the stranger nods reassuringly.

"Well, how *long* do I have to stay here to get the deal?"

"Fifteen years."

***

Now, I want you to ask yourself: If you received such an offer what would you do? Accept it? Reject it? Ask to see the genie's credentials?

Let me tell you what *I* think you would do.

I think you'd say "Forget it!"

Most people don't want to be imprisoned for 15 years, even in their own homes. Most individuals would *never* give up their freedom for such a long time, even in exchange for all the creature comforts they could possibly want.

That being the case, then please consider this: Most adults will spend approximately 45 years in the workplace (they will start work when they reach 20–25 years of age and retire when they are 65–70). Furthermore, about a third of every working adult's life (8 hours a day) will be spent in work-related pursuits (transport to and from work, working, bringing work home to finish). When people actually add up all the work-related hours they spend during a week (even assuming they have the weekend off), a total of 56 hours (8 hours a day) is common. Thus, a person who lives long enough to reach retirement will have spent approximately one third of his or her adult life (8 hours a day for 45 years) in the workplace. That adds up to 15 years spent on the job.

Now here's the irony: The same people who would *never* voluntarily remain imprisoned in their own homes for 15 years (even when plied with all the free amenities and creature comforts they want) *will* voluntarily remain imprisoned in a job they don't like for 15 years of their adult lives—and they don't even get all the free benefits thrown in with the "house arrest" offer!

This is obviously a tragic situation. People should not spend a third of their adult lives in activity they find unrewarding, unsatisfying, or worse, even distasteful. Talk about a loss of quality time! How can you effectively *Romance the Clock* and ever hope to love your time on Earth when a third of it is spent in various shades of misery.

WHAT IF YOU ENJOY YOUR JOB?

If you happen to be among those fortunate persons who *like* their work, who enjoy the job they are performing, then I have good news. You don't have to read this chapter. Go directly to Action Step 7. Why? Because if you are finding meaning and satisfaction in your workplace you are already *Romancing the Clock*—even if it is a punch clock!

Conversely, if you're the kind of employee who needs to celebrate "Hump Night" (Wednesday) because you're "over the hump" and on the way to the weekend—if you're the kind of worker who sees work as a "four-letter word"—then I hope you'll read on.

MAKING YOUR WORKPLACE A WORTHPLACE

Hans Selye, the famous endocrinologist, was often referred to as the "Father of Stress" because he did so much to help us understand how stress works and what it does to the human body.

Selye was also known for his long workdays. He was once asked how he could work 17-hour days—day in, day out—and still remain healthy. He answered that if you *enjoy* your work, then doing it 17 hours a day won't cause stress; however, if you work 3 or 4 hours a day at a job you can't stand, that can be very stressful! It's not the time you spend in the job, then, that determines how stressful it will be, but whether you like or dislike what you are doing.

What every person should strive for is to find a job (career) that will provide *meaningful, satisfying* work—an occupation in which he or she can both *earn a living* and achieve *personal satisfaction* at the same time. When this happens, the workplace becomes a WORTHplace; a place where economic and personal goals are both achieved. Enjoying your life's work goes a long way toward accentuating positives and reducing negatives (hassles) in your life.

WHAT CAN I DO—RIGHT NOW—TO INCREASE THE CHANCES THAT I WILL FIND SATISFACTION IN THE WORK I PERFORM?

One of the most critical steps you can take is to be *proactive* (rather than reactive) in your job/profession/career choice. Being proactive rather than reactive means you don't just "fall" into a job . . . *you think about what you want from your life and then you choose the kind of work that will help you achieve your life's ambitions (goals).* The sooner you begin this process of deciding what you want out of life and the type of work that can get you that kind of life, the better your chances will be of finding a meaningful, personally satisfying workplace in the years to come. (And, of course, the sooner you find the right workplace, the longer you will have to enjoy working there!)

I have a self-assessment exercise that will help you find the workplace that is right for you. It is called the Aspiration–Occupation (A–O) Exercise. The purpose of the A–O Exercise is to help you discover whether your current plans and activities will help you meet your long-term goals and objectives in life.

Before you begin the exercise, consider this incredible paradox. As thinking, mature adults, most of us *plan* for things that make a difference in our lives. For example, very few of us would consider taking a long automobile trip without first considering where we want to go and the best route to reach our destination. Yet, when it comes to the one thing that makes an incredible difference in our lives—our career—we give precious little thought to the destination we want to reach before we set off on that all-important journey down the road of life. This is an unfortunate paradox, indeed! Unfortunate because it is much easier to alter career objectives and change educational programs while you are young than 5, 10, or 15 years down the wrong career path, when family and/or financial obligations make it difficult to shift gears and set off in a new direction—particularly if it requires extensive retooling or retraining.

Thus, it is critical that each of us consider what our ultimate goals in life are *early on*, and assess whether our current actions (e.g., preparation for a specific job or working in a specific job) will provide us with the best route to achieving those goals. If you haven't yet considered what your ultimate goals are, don't despair; it's never too late to consider the issue. My recommendation, however, would be to do it *now* (or as soon as possible). By answering the questions that follow, you should be in a better position to make that assessment.

THE ASPIRATION–OCCUPATION EXERCISE

Instructions

In completing the A–O Exercise, please keep the following points in mind:

1. The A–O Exercise can be helpful regardless of your age when you take it. It is most useful when taken before preparing for your first career, because it is easier to make changes in your plans and achieve greater long-term benefits from choosing the "right" career at this stage in your life. However, *USA Today* recently reported that college graduates can expect to have an average of three different careers and 10 jobs in their lifetimes! This means that in the contemporary work world it is possible (and more acceptable than in the past) to make career changes later in life. This exercise can be beneficial even for people in their thirties, forties, and beyond.

2. Take your time in answering the questions. Don't rush. Consider each inquiry *before* you write down your answer. If you need more space than provided here, feel free to use additional paper.

3. There is no "right" or "wrong" answer to any question in this exercise, but there *is* a *best* answer. The best answer is the answer that best expresses the way you truly feel about the item at this point in your life.

4. Once you have recorded your answers, read them to see what direction they are pointing toward concerning what you want out of life and what you might want to do to achieve your objectives.

5. In doing the A–O Exercise, it is important to remember that the answers you give today might change in the years to come. Therefore, it is important to redo the exercise every few years to make sure that your Aspirations (your goals in life) and Occupation (your career) are still in "sync" or harmony.

The Questions

1a. What are the things you want most out of life?

1b. Is the job you are in (or considering) giving you the opportunity to achieve these things? Why or why not?

2a. If you could design your own job—one that was exactly what you wanted—how would that job description read?

2b. How does your "ideal" job description compare with your current (or contemplated) job description?

3a. Most people have one or more activities that have interested them throughout a major portion of their lives. Can you think of any such activities that have been a part of your life? List them.

3b. Are any of these activities incorporated (involved) in your current or contemplated occupation?

4a. Pretend that you have just won the lottery and find yourself financially secure for the rest of your life. Now that you have financial independence and don't ever have to earn an income to live comfortably, what would you want to do with the rest of your life? Make a list of the activity(ies) you would pursue.

4b. Do your current plans and/or occupation give you a chance to do the activity(ies) you listed in question 4a? (Hopefully, they do. The ideal Aspiration–Occupation match is achieved when a person would continue doing the same job even when he or she didn't have to.)

4c. If your answer to question 4b was "No," can you think of any other kind of work that you would still want to do—even if you were financially independent and weren't required to do it for a living?

4d. If you answered question 4c and were able to come up with a different type of work, is it worth it for you to try and pursue that type of work as a new career in your life? In answering this question, list the pros and cons of pursuing this new career (job opportunities, training time, cost, family obligations, etc). If, after weighing the pros and cons, you feel that pursuing the new career is worth it, try to come up with an action plan that might help you achieve entry into that job field. (In developing this action plan you might need to solicit help from other people; for instance, career counselors, loved ones, employees already in that line of work.)

WHAT ARE MY OPTIONS IF I'M STUCK IN A JOB I DON'T REALLY ENJOY?

All right. You've completed the A–O Exercise and discovered that the job you're in is not where you want to be. Or maybe you knew that already and the A–O Exercise has helped you pinpoint where you *should* be. What are your options at this point? Basically, you have three choices:

1. *You can remain in the job you have and do nothing to try and improve it.* This option is the least desirable because it leaves you in the untenable position of spending a third of your life doing something you don't enjoy, which can be hazardous to your mental and physical well-being. I don't recommend it.

2. *You can try to modify your current job to make it more palatable.* This is a less radical option than option 3, which follows, and may very well be the best choice for those individuals who can make enough changes in their jobs to make them reasonably satisfying. This approach will also appeal to those who fear quitting their current jobs because of their age, financial resources, lack of skills, or lack of desire to "retool" (retrain) for a new career. We will discuss this second option in a moment.

3. *You can change your job or career.* This is the most drastic option and should be considered only as a last resort. Yet, under certain conditions, it is an *appropriate* option. We will discuss this choice at the end of the chapter.

HOW TO MODIFY YOUR CURRENT JOB TO MAKE IT A MORE POSITIVE WORK EXPERIENCE

Sometimes it is just not possible to change jobs, even though it means that your aspirations and your occupation are out of step. But does that leave you with *no* alternatives to improving the quality of your work life? Fear not! Even though you can't change your job you still might be able to change what you do *in* your job to make it more personally satisfying.

How is this possible?

By doing what you can to accentuate the positive and reduce the negative aspects of your job.

When I speak with people who don't like their work I always ask them: *Is everything about your work terrible, or are there some aspects of your job that are more enjoyable than others?* Most individuals, upon reflection, will admit that it isn't the "whole" job that is bad, but rather, certain aspects of it.

Consider your own work situation. I presume you aren't happy with your employment or you wouldn't be reading this chapter. Yet, before you condemn your job as a total "loser" get out a pen and pencil and list *any* parts of your job that you find acceptable or even enjoyable. Also write down those things about the job you don't like doing, that make the work unpleasant.

Here is what I think you will discover. When you think of the *total* job in *general* terms it will appear more undesirable than if you divide it into its component parts, some of which will be favorable and some unfavorable.

If this turns out to be true, if some parts of your job are more enjoyable than other parts, then you have an opening to improve the overall quality of your worklife.

WORK TO ACCENTUATE THE POSITIVE AND REDUCE THE NEGATIVE PARTS OF YOUR JOB

What you want to do is attempt to *modify* your job to reduce the bad parts and expand the good parts. Sometimes this can be accomplished by simply talking with your boss and seeing if you can spend more time doing what you enjoy at work and less time doing what you find disagreeable. Your boss might be very amenable to this, particularly if you perform the work you enjoy well and he or she can find a way to assign the work you don't enjoy to someone else who doesn't mind doing it. Sometimes you can bypass your boss completely and (if allowable) barter parts of your job with peers, swapping tasks so that both parties get rid of tasks they don't like and end up with tasks they enjoy. (Hopefully you work with colleagues who have complementary tastes in work.) If you are self-employed, you can farm out those aspects of your work that cause you hassle (see Action Step 2) and *pay* someone else to do the tasks for you.

By analyzing your job you might discover that it is not the *work* you dislike but, rather, the people you work with. Maybe you are having problems with your supervisor or a colleague. If that is the case, transferring to another part of the organization (if it is large enough) or taking a similar job at a competing organization may solve your problem.

I recall the case of a real estate agent who was very unhappy with her job because she didn't like the broker who ran the office where she worked. She requested and received a transfer to a different office with the same company—and worked happily ever after.

WATCH OUT FOR THE "B FACTOR" IN YOUR WORK AND IN YOUR LIFE

There is one other aspect of work that can influence the way you feel about your job. I call it the "B Factor." "B" *stands for* "Boredom," and it is vital to become aware of it so that (a) you can recognize it if it begins to affect your job satisfaction and (b) you can take steps to counteract its negative impact in your worklife.

Let me introduce this factor with a personal story. Several years ago I was on a promotional tour, appearing on various radio and television programs to discuss a book I had written. Most of these programs were talk shows, involving 10 to 15 minutes of discussion between the host and myself. It was a comfortable, easygoing format. There was one exception, however: Somehow I had been scheduled to discuss my book on a morning "top forty" show—the kind with a disc jockey who plays rock music to legions of fans. The idea of discussing my book between hit records, weather reports, and local ad spots—all at the hyperspeed preferred by disc jockeys—was a trifle disconcerting, but I knew it would be worth it. You see, I spent most of my youth dreaming about becoming a disc jockey, and now, at last, I was going to meet one face to face.

And at first I wasn't disappointed. In fact, I was so fascinated with the disc jockey and his control room antics that I hardly remember the actual program. Afterward he invited me to lunch in the station's cafeteria. I gladly accepted. We ate at a small table by ourselves, and I waited patiently until he was finished before I asked him *the* question.

"Tell me," I asked, "How does it feel?"

He looked at me blankly. "What do you mean?"

"How does it *really* feel to be a disc jockey?"

His expression didn't change.

I decided to elaborate. "I mean, how does it feel to be right in the center of things—with rock stars on one side, and the fans on the other—and you right in the middle of the action?"

The disc jockey—my hero—stared straight ahead with tired eyes and shattered my little illusion with one verbal shot. "It feels boring," he said flatly. "All I want to do is go home and go sailing." And with that he nodded good-bye and walked out of the cafeteria.

I sat, stunned, for several minutes before I got up and headed for the exit. On my way out I passed an observation window where I could see the afternoon disc jockey spinning records and talking into his microphone. I stopped to watch his frantic activity and then it hit me: Yes, it would be great to be a disc jockey for a while—a year, maybe two—but then how interesting would it be to sit in a little cubicle and tout the local pizza palace while spinning little discs on a turntable and making the weather sound as exciting as the play-by-play of the superbowl? Not very exciting at all, I decided, and I began to understand what my host had meant about boredom a few minutes before.

You know, boredom is a very important factor in the human condition. It can motivate us to expand our horizons as we seek new kinds of stimulation; yet it can also be the "rust of human emotion," leading to dissatisfaction with people, jobs, and activities as we become used to them.

Let us consider boredom and its relationship to work. Any job, no matter what kind it is, has the potential to become boring if it remains basically the same over a long period of time. This is because as we learn a job, the skills that were once a challenge become automatic, and the things that were novel and exciting when we started work become mundane and predictable after being repeated day after day.

How *fast* a job becomes boring will vary, depending in part on the complexity of the job, how much the job changes over time, the personality of the employee, and the skills of the manager in keeping the employee satisfied and productive. (I have often heard a worker comment: "I'd quit this boring job if it weren't for my manager.")

Only recently have behavioral scientists begun to recognize the significance of boredom in affecting worker satisfaction and productivity. To combat this motivation crippler, they have devised an antidote: *job enrichment*. They have studied the effectiveness of this antidote in the workplace, usually on assembly-line jobs, where the repetitive, relatively simple tasks invite boredom.

Do not think, however, that the assembly line is the only place where boredom can strike with devastating results. It can affect doctors, accountants, and engineers, too. Any job, over time, can lose its luster. This is critical: *Any* job has the potential to become boring if a person stays in it long enough and/or the work doesn't change. And that goes for blue-collar work, white-collar work, unskilled labor, professional work, and—yes—executive-level work, too. No one is immune.

As a worker what can you do about boredom? How can you combat this potentially destructive factor and keep your satisfaction and productivity high? You can use job enrichment when possible; that is, when such enrichment is allowed by the organization and existing contractual obligations. Here are two steps to take in combating boredom in *your* job:

1. *Watch for the telltale signs of boredom in your work.* If you have been assigned to a specific job for a long time, and if that job is relatively easy for you to master, then the possibility of boredom increases. Watch for warning signals, such as listlessness on the job, increasing work complaints, more frequent absenteeism, and a loss of morale in the workplace. One of the most reliable telltale signs of boredom is what I call the "gradual decay function" in job performance. It is not a sudden drop-off in productivity—that is more likely to be caused by specific factors such as illness, momentary unhappiness with some aspect of the workplace, or a personal crisis. The *boredom factor* produces a more gradual decay in performance, like putting on weight slowly, over a long period of time.

2. *Use job enrichment to combat boredom on the job.* The best way to stave off the relentless assault of workplace boredom is to expand your job

responsibilities at a rate that keeps you challenged but not over-whelmed. Thus, as you master job skills, additional or different ones can be assigned. Sometimes this means expanding your specific job to include new responsibilities and skills; other times it means being promoted to a new job. In either case, the emphasis is on giving yourself job enrichment to maintain and fend off boredom in the workplace.

Boredom is not enjoyable; people normally strive to avoid or eliminate it. You should not hesitate, then, to seek out job enrichment if you see yourself getting in a rut where your work is losing its challenge and stimulation.

In most larger organizations there are numerous job enrichment programs you can take advantage of in your battle against boredom. Some require additional education or training programs, which in themselves help combat boredom. Here are some job enrichment approaches you might consider to help combat boredom on the job. Whichever ones you choose should be adapted to your particular work circumstances for maximum effectiveness.

- On some jobs (for instance, on assembly lines) it is possible to rotate through several types of jobs, thus relieving the boredom of doing the same task time after time.
- You can expand your job to encompass new skills and responsibilities.
- You can seek a promotion that may require new challenges and skills to stimulate workplace interest.
- You can seek out new colleagues to work with.

Before leaving the topic of job boredom in particular, and job satisfaction in general, I'd like to close with two final observations:

First, it is sometimes tempting to look at certain kinds of jobs—particularly repetitive ones like those on assembly lines—and automatically label them boring. Don't make this mistake. A job that seems boring to one person might be perfectly satisfying and even highly challenging to someone else; this depends to a great degree on the ability of the person performing the task in question. There are always some individuals who enjoy doing the very jobs that others would find boring the minute they walk in the door.

When it comes to determining whether you are bored, don't focus on the kind of work you do, but on the way you feel about that work as you perform it over the length of your career.

Second, it helps to understand boredom on the job by comparing it to the problem of boredom that occurs in long-term interpersonal relationships, particularly marriages. Think of what happens when you first begin work on a new job or embark on a new interpersonal relationship such as marriage: Everything is exciting, novel, stimulating—like a new car or a Christmas toy. But what happens after a significant period of time has passed? What was once exciting, novel, and stimulating has the potential of becoming predictable, mundane, and even stultifying. In short, the novelty has worn off and the initial exhilaration you once felt is now replaced by a feeling of "I've done all this before." To keep your enthusiasm about a job or a marriage alive and vibrant you must *work* at it—constantly expanding your experiences and activities to keep boredom at bay!

That's a great way to love your time on Earth—and your job and your spouse along with it.

THE MOST DRASTIC OPTION: DEALING WITH JOB DISSATISFACTION BY SEEKING NEW EMPLOYMENT

As I pointed out earlier, if you are seriously dissatisfied with your job, then you have three alternatives. You can stay at the job—spend at least 8 hours a day being unhappy—and risk the medical dangers associated with excessive stress (see Action Step 10). You can try to maintain your present position but alter what you do to make it more interesting and in line with your life goals (the option just discussed). If this is not possible, you can attempt to change jobs or careers.

Obviously, changing careers is not something to be taken lightly. But, then, neither is a lifetime spent at distressful labor. Dr. David Fink recognizes the importance of changing directions in life. He recommends making a fresh start "if your life has led you into a detour that is taking you where you do not want to go." He goes on to say:

> It may be tough; tomorrow it will be tougher, because you will be that much farther away from your destination. . . . To many, this advice to redirect your own life will sound somehow subversive, radical, and dangerous. Nothing could be farther from the truth. If you want to subvert your life, to undermine it radically, live it against the direction of the flow of your real personality. If your job makes you sick, quit it. What difference does it make how good it is if it isn't good for you?

No job is going to be joyous and fulfilling all the time; and the decision to make a change should not be based on petty annoyances or momentary fits of pique. There is a line between the trials and tribulations at work and the tragedy of unfulfilling work. If you feel you have crossed over that line, Dr. Fink suggests you take five steps:

1. Make a list of your talents and skills.

2. Ask yourself what kind of work would give you an opportunity to exercise those talents and skills.

3. Pick that vocation within your scope which will furnish the most satisfactions.

4. Make a decision, and get started. If you need further training, that is priority number one.

5. All of your old activities and habits that do not fit in with your new purpose are out for the duration.

In making a final decision concerning something as critical as changing your employment and/or career you need to balance current realities—the job market, the problem of credentials, financial considerations—against the realities of an unsatisfying job—the high potential for poor health, unfulfilled needs, and the tragic loss of time in your life.

Should you make such a move? Take stock of where you are, carefully analyzing your own particular circumstances, and you will be in a better position to determine which course of action to take. One manager put it this way: "Work to your heart's content; but if your heart isn't in your work, then your heart may very well put you out of work."

Something to think about.

Revel in the Journey or Skip the Trip!

I first met Tony back in the 1970s when he was in my psychology class at the City University of New York. Because I taught a large lecture class of more than 300, I didn't get a chance to know many of my students on an in-dividual basis.

Tony was an exception. He would come up to see me during my office hours and ask me about course assignments and testing procedures. Mostly, however, he talked to me about writing books. He knew I was a published author and he wanted to "pick my brain" about job opportunities for profes-sional writers.

"Making a living as a full-time writer is somewhere between difficult and next-to-impossible," I cautioned him. "You usually need some other type of job to support you while you do writing on the side."

That didn't satisfy Tony. "I want a career in writing," he assured me. "My goal is to have the number one book on the New York Times best-seller list someday."

"Well, at least you don't think small," I chuckled. "But let me warn you: There are only a few best-selling authors out there . . . less than one percent of the profession. The rest of the people who make writing a full-time career end up scratching just to make ends meet. For them, writing is not glamorous *or* lucrative . . . just a lot of hard work, frequent rejections, and infrequent paychecks."

My warnings fell on deaf ears. "I know it will be a *challenge*," Tony admitted. "But it's what I *want* to do."

Tony and I lost touch with each other after he graduated and I left New York to seek warmer climes in Florida. Every once in a while I would think of him when I read the book review section of my local newspaper. I wondered whether he ever pursued the writing life or decided to give it up for more lucrative pursuits.

Then, in the late 1990s I had a chance encounter with Tony during one of my visits to New York City. He happened to be attending a convention at the hotel where I was staying and was seated across from me at lunch. It had been 30 years since I had last seen him, and, had it not been for a name tag he was wearing, I wouldn't have recognized him. He had put on some weight since our last encounter, and his hairline had retreated to the edge of baldness.

After recovering from the surprise of our unexpected reunion, Tony and I set about filling each other in on what had been happening in our lives since we last met.

"What about your plans to be a full-time writer?" I inquired. "Did you stick with your plans?"

"Yes," Tony assured me. "It's been almost 30 years now." He paused and looked at me for a moment. "You were right about the profession, though."

"How . . .?"

"It isn't easy from a financial standpoint. It's been a struggle to keep ahead of the bills since day one."

I gave an understanding nod. "You're not alone, that I can assure you."

"I keep hoping for that one *big* book to put me over the top."

I studied the expression on Tony's face. I could discern neither hope nor resignation. "Tell me," I asked, "how do you feel about writing now; I mean, after all this time—all the effort—and still no number one best-seller."

Tony's face took on a wistful look. "I always thought I'd reach my goal of having a best-seller, but truthfully, I don't see that happening now. Don't get me wrong," he hastily added, "I'm not about to stop trying at this late date, but I'm realistic enough to figure that if it hasn't happened in almost 30 years it's probably not going to happen in the next 30, either—if I live that long."

"You still seem enthusiastic about writing, though," I had to admit, impressed by his description of how he worked at his craft day after day.

"That's the beauty of it, you see," he confided. Tony took the napkin that was next to his plate and unfolded it. "Imagine that this is a blank piece of paper."

"Okay," I agreed.

"Every day I go into my study and face a blank piece of paper. My challenge is to fill that paper with my own words, something meaningful. It's me against the empty page. I'm in control of my own destiny: If I don't write well, there's no one to blame but myself. If I do create something of value, then I'm the one who deserves the credit. I've always loved writing—that's why I've spent a lifetime doing it. Writing is my passion. I *have* to do it. That's the point. Success or failure is important, but it is of secondary importance to the act of writing itself. Writing is what gives me joy and meaning in life. If I ever do achieve my goal of a number one best-seller, well, that would just be frosting on the cake."

I congratulated Tony on his perseverance and encouraged him to stay the course.

Along with a sense of joy, I also felt an overwhelming sense of *relief* for my one-time student, because I knew Tony had discovered a great truth when it comes to *Romancing the Clock* and loving your time on this Earth.

Tony had learned to:

Revel in the journey or skip the trip!

Certainly, the achievement of his goal—a number one best-seller would have made Tony happy, but—and this is an important "but"—because his main love in life was the act of writing, it was not necessary to achieve the goal to satisfy (or justify) his time spent pursuing it. His life would not be wasted if he didn't get that best-seller, because it was the *journey* (the act of writing), not the *destination* (the best-seller) that gave meaning and worth to what he did with his life and *why* he did it.

For those people who define their success or failure in life purely on the basis of whether they achieve or fail to achieve their goal(s); for those individuals who think only in terms of the *destination* and not the *journey*, a harsh reality awaits. And it is this: Many people who set long-term goals for themselves will spend a lifetime pusuing them without success. They will *fail* to achieve their goals, particularly if the goals they set were so difficult to achieve that failure was almost assured from the outset.

Now, if the *only* reason a person pursued a long-term activity (a job, a task, an education, an apprenticeship) was to achieve an objective or goal, then what happens if that objective or goal is not reached?

The person feels an overwhelming sense of failure and believes that a large portion of life has been wasted.

That is why you should never pursue an objective or goal in life if your only satisfaction will come in achieving that objective or goal. The goal or objective, rather than being the *main* reason you undertake an activity, should be a kind of "bonus" or "collateral benefit" that comes from participating in an activity that you *enjoy for its own sake.*

Recall what Tony, my student turned writer, said about his career: "I've always loved writing. That's why I've spent a lifetime doing it . . . Success or failure is important, but it is of secondary importance to the act of writing itself. Writing is what gives me joy and meaning in life. If I ever do achieve my goal of a number one best-seller, well, that would just be frosting on the cake."

Revel in the journey, or skip the trip!

This is a recommendation worth remembering as you prepare to undertake a long-term activity of your own. Life holds no guarantees, no iron-clad promises of success in the activities you pursue. But if you *enjoy* what you are doing, if you revel in the journey, then you will love the time you spend on your trip, even if you don't travel quite as far as you had hoped you would.

SELECTING YOUR CAREER: REVEL IN THAT JOURNEY, TOO!

What is the best way to guarantee personal satisfaction in life when it comes to choosing the right job? Sadly, there is no way to guarantee personal happiness. But I do believe that the best chance you have to enjoy life and, at the same time, succeed in your chosen career, is to *revel in the journey, or skip the trip.*

Why is this?

Because, as with Tony the writer, there is no guarantee that what you want is what you'll end up getting. Therefore:

The pursuit of a goal is sometimes as important as achievement of the goal itself—if not more so.

Let me provide you with one final example of what I'm trying to emphasize here. It involves . . .

A GYMNAST IN SEARCH OF GOLD

When my daughter was young, she decided to participate in gymnastics. It didn't take her long to learn that this particular sport is one of the most demanding, grueling activities ever created to test the limits of human endurance and skill. Participants are expected to display a fierce dedication to their sport, committing long hours of practice, day after day, year after year, to perfecting their talent. Most gymnasts who "make it" start at an early age, some as young as two or three, and most are considered "over the hill" by the time they are old enough to drink legally. As far as a normal childhood is concerned, you can forget it: These athletes eat, sleep, and breathe their sport. Gymnastics *is* their life.

My daughter had no desire to pursue gymnastics with such fierce intensity and commitment; to her it was an opportunity to keep fit and enjoy a challenging workout on a regular basis. But she shared with me an interesting story she had read about one gymnast who *was* driven to achieve stardom in the sport, and who set his sights on the ultimate gymnastic prize: an Olympic gold medal.

This young man exhibited a fanatic devotion to his goal. He pushed relentlessly toward his objective, through long hours, through pain, through years spent in the gym. His skill and dedication were about to pay off. He looked like a serious contender for victory at the next Olympic games.

And then the unthinkable happened. The U.S. government decided to boycott the 1980 Olympic Games, denying the young man the chance to realize his dream of achieving an Olympic gold medal.

Now I ask you to consider this: If the only thing that mattered to this dedicated gymnast was achieving his goal of an Olympic victory, then what could one say about the time he had devoted to his sport?

That it was wasted.

On the other hand, if the young man *enjoyed* doing gymnastics—if he felt positive about the activities he undertook to prepare for international competition—then his efforts were not wasted.

Why? Because he *enjoyed the journey* he took on his way to the Olympics. The fact that he never actually achieved his goal, although disappointing, was not disastrous. Like Tony the author, who has enjoyed a lifetime of writing books that might never become best-sellers, the young athlete found joy and quality time in the pursuit of his dream.

***

Life is short. Objectives are not always met, goals not always achieved. Consider this when you travel through life. Choose your route carefully. There are many roads you could follow. Pick those where you can revel in the journey, or skip the trip. That's the best way to have the *time of your life!*

Don't Always Put Off Until Tomorrow What You Can Enjoy Today

I guess you could consider my brother-in-law Shel to be the typical American guy of his time. He worked hard at his insurance job, liked sports, smoked and ate a bit too much, and was a wizard at the backyard barbecue. In fact, his barbecued ribs were so good—and I bragged about them so much—that friends believed I flew all the way from Florida to Minnesota just to taste those succulent goodies. Of course, the *real* reason I made the flight was to visit the family, but I can't deny that those tender, tasty, honey-brushed, lean and meaty ribs helped speed me on my way!

I recall one visit in particular. It was a Sunday afternoon during early October, one of those crisp, clear fall days splashed with the color of falling leaves and the sounds of restless birds; the kind of autumn day that made you forget that the promise of a Minnesota autumn is the curse of a Minnesota winter soon to follow.

I was seated at a picnic table in my brother-in-law's backyard, eating racks of ribs as fast as they were deposited on my plate. My sister and mom were there, too, but unlike Shel and me, their major focus was on conversation, not consumption. That meant that the women did most of the talking and we did most of the eating, which was fine with me. At the end of the dinner, I found that my gluttony had rendered me incapable of movement. I stretched out in my chair and, without additional food to distract me, I turned my attention to the discussion that preceded the arrival of dessert.

Shel's 44th birthday was coming soon and he was registering his annual complaint about how he still hadn't had the opportunity to visit Las Vegas.

"I told you I'd go with you whenever you want," I reminded him. "I made the same offer *last* year."

Shel acknowledged the gesture. "I know, it's just been so damn busy at the office. Every time I get ready to go, some emergency pops up."

"Are you sure you want to go that badly?" I eyed him directly, trying to gauge the level of his desire from his facial expression.

"Yes! I've waited a lifetime to go on that trip."

He *looked* convincing.

"Well, then, what are we waiting for? Let's make plans *now*."

Shel rose from his seat and walked over to my side of the table. "I can't make it this year," he said regretfully, "I'm up to my neck in casework."

"That's what you said last year," I reminded him.

"Okay, but next year will be different. I'll make sure. I promise you we'll do it next year." He extended his hand. "Let's shake on it."

"You've got a deal," I agreed, and we shook on it.

Problem was, there was no next year for Shel. He was diagnosed with cancer and died before his 45th birthday.

SHEL'S LEGACY

Whenever I hear someone say "I'll do such-and-such a thing next year," I always think of Shel and I'm reminded that none of us are ever guaranteed a "next year" or even a "next week."

Shel put off an activity he badly wanted to do because he assumed he had unlimited time to make it happen. He was mistaken.

Don't you be.

When it comes to undertaking an activity you really want to do, do it.

Some might see this viewpoint as being somewhat selfish and irresponsible. After all, is not the ability to postpone gratification the hallmark of being a responsible, mature adult? Yes, to a point. I'm not suggesting that a person chuck his family and job and head for some tropical paradise to live out a fantasy of sun, surf, and sand. Nor am I recommending adultery, murder, or embezzlement as a means of getting what you want.

What I *am* saying is that we need to live lives that are more than responsibility *without* reward. The standard phrase I am echoing here is "We need to stop and smell the roses." The specific recommendation I am making is that we find a balance in our lives between doing what we are expected to do as responsible adults and doing what we *enjoy* doing as *Romancers of the Clock.*

There is nothing wrong with taking a break.

With taking that long-awaited vacation.

With saying "It's time to do something for *me.*"

For each of us there is a continuum of behavior that runs from *selfless* to *selfish* behavior. When we are selfless we give too much of ourselves and expect too little from others; when we are selfish we give too little of ourselves and expect too much from others. Both ends of the continuum are unhealthy.

We need to achieve a balance between doing things for ourselves and for others, giving of ourselves, and giving to ourselves. It is this balance that creates the greatest joy of living and the greatest joy of giving.

Make an effort to achieve that balance within yourself and you will be taking an important step in loving your time on Earth.

THE QUESTION OF CHILDREN

When it comes to the *"We'll do it next year . . ."* strategy, nothing seems to be postponed more frequently than having children in our contemporary get-married-later, two-career-couple world.

Whether this is an appropriate strategy depends, of course, on each couple's circumstances and needs. One couple we know waited until their mid-forties to have their first child, saying they wanted to postpone parenthood so they could establish their careers, have some time together, and accumulate enough wealth so that children would not prove a financial hardship. Fifteen years later, well into parenthood, they stood by the correctness of their strategy but did admit that having children at an earlier age would have "given them more energy to deal with the demands children make on parents." In other words, this particular father and mother were finding it difficult to keep up with their kids, whether it was driving them all over town or staving off medical nightmares (muscle and ligament trauma, heart and lung problems) during backyard basketball games.

What about you? Are you planning to have children? The key word here is "planning." Bringing a child into this world is the *single most critical long-term time-impacting event you will experience in your life* (assuming, of course, that you intend to be a parent and not an absentee biological breeding agent).

For that reason, decisions about whether and when to have children become critical parenting issues worthy of careful consideration.

Having children should never be a casual or spur-of-the-moment decision. Once you have children, it's too late to decide that they are too much of a hassle. Unlike my dad's boat (see Action Step 1), which could be disposed of when it became too great a liability, you can't return kids to their original embryonic state. Biology doesn't work that way. Nor is it fair to turn them into "latchkey" children, for whom parents provide little more than custodial care as they invest themselves and their time in their careers or other adults rather than their families.

If you end up loving your children as much as I do mine, then it will be extremely difficult to put off until tomorrow (childbirth) what you can enjoy today. The ticking of the biological clock can become deafening. So can the pleadings of would-be grandmothers.

As was the case with my brother-in-law Shel's trip to Las Vegas, I wouldn't put off children for *too* long if you want them, even in today's society, where establishing and maintaining personal and financial freedom for as long as possible seems to dictate that families be started later in life—if at all. What I *would* do, however, is fully understand the responsibilities and obligations you are undertaking when you bring a child into this complex world of ours. You are (or should be) making a lifelong commitment of time and energy to your son(s) and/or daughter (s).

Sadly, in our contemporary world, many people are not ready to make that commitment and still have children. They make the grievous error of failing to understand the difference between biological reproduction and parenthood. Even sadder, it is the children of these parents who suffer the most from that lack of commitment—the children, and the society in which they live.

If you aren't willing to commit yourself and your time to your children, you shouldn't be a parent.

Period.

I know that sounds harsh, but so are the consequences that arise when biological fathers and mothers aren't *parents*.

A strong, loving, committed family is the basic building block of a healthy, vigorous, morally robust country.

You, as a parent or parent-to-be, can do your part to ensure the future health of your children, your nation, and your Earth.

Isn't it about *time* that you did?

Avoid the Pitfalls of Perfectionism

Many years ago, before the advent of the personal computer made difficult manuscript corrections a thing of the past, I had a colleague who was a perfectionist when it came to her writing. She was a brilliant thinker and talented author, yet, she was never able to produce the volume of work one would have expected from a person with her exceptional skills.

Why?

Because she was a *perfectionist*.

If she typed a page with one error, she retyped it.

If she typed a page with a less-than-perfect erasure, she retyped it.

If she re-read a page and decided a word could be changed for more impact, she retyped it.

One time when she misnumbered a 50 page manuscript, she retyped every page and renumbered it.

This woman was known to have gone through five, six, even ten revisions of a manuscript before deeming it adequate for submission to a journal or publisher.

Needless to say, she spent most of her time *correcting* her compositions rather than *creating* them. The end result: Instead of taking a week to complete a manuscript, this professor would take months or *more*.

And here's the sad part: 10 percent of her time accounted for about 90 percent of her project's ultimate worth. The other 90 percent was spent in "fine-tuning" it. In her attempt to make the project *perfect*, she had basically wasted 90 percent of her overall effort. She had actually "one-upped" the old "80-20 rule," which states that 20 percent of the people do 80 percent of the work. She was now functioning under the "90-10 rule" which indicated that 10 percent of her effort was creating 90 percent of her work.

Such is the problem and the danger of perfectionism in our lives.

IS BEING PERFECT REALLY NECESSARY?

Here is the truth when it comes to "perfection." There are very few times when perfection is required to gain all the benefits you need from your labors. Yet it is the difference between performing competently and perfectly that wastes much of our time and robs us of much of our enjoyment in the tasks we perform.

Consider, for example, academic grades. To graduate from most universities with top honors requires approximately an even number of "A's" and "B's" on a student's grade transcript (a 3.5 grade-point average out of a possible 4.0). That is to say, a student with a 3.5 average will get all the benefits of a student with a perfect, straight-A, 4.0 average. Now, if you ask any student (or professor) where the most extra time must be spent in achieving good grades, it is in the difference between an "A" and a "B."

Considering this information, I often ask students who are striving for straight-A averages why they are spending *so* much additional time getting those extra "A's" when they could settle for more "B's," get the same graduation benefits, and use that extra time to do other things (like build up their extracurricular activities, increase their business experience, or just have time for more fun).

The student will usually respond with an answer like "Well, I want to do my best."

That's a good, "I'm not a quitter," answer. But when doing your best means doing much *better* than you have to and spending a lot more time achieving such an objective, you might begin to question the wisdom of such an approach.

IS BEING PERFECT REALLY WORTH IT?

Think of your own life in these terms. Are you a *perfectionist?* Are there things you could do *well* in a short time but that you choose instead to do *perfectly* in a much longer period of time? Does the extra time justify the difference? Is the difference really that necessary?

I have a neighbor who (gasp!) maintains his own lawn. I've watched him do it during my cardiovascular walks around the block. It takes him about 90 minutes to cut the grass and then *an additional hour and a half* to make slight cosmetic trimming adjustments that are hardly noticeable to the naked eye. In other words, he cuts his lawn competently in half the time that it takes him to cut his lawn *perfectly*. Again, is it worth it?

When you start thinking about your own behavior I think you will be amazed to see how often you are caught up in a perfectionistic frenzy and how many times you waste time doing jobs perfectly that could be performed competently with no significant loss in quality or function.

There are times when the need to do something perfectly is rooted in psychological problems. Obsessive-compulsive behavior, for example, often leads one to behave in ways which mimic the need to do things perfectly. To illustrate, individuals with OCD (obsessive-compulsive disorder) might wash their hands four or five times when once will do.

There are also times when the need for perfection is rooted in our belief that such behavior is desirable and proof of good moral character. "Practice makes perfect," as the old saying goes. That is true, but is it *necessary?* A more appropriate saying, based on a more enjoyable and economical use of time, might be "Practice makes perfect, but competence practiced makes perfect sense."

DO YOU SUFFER FROM "PERFECTIONITIS?"

Just for the fun of it, I'm going to write down a list of things (activities) that most people do. Think of the way you do them. Think of the way other people do them. Ask yourself: What is the difference between doing these tasks *competently* and doing them *perfectly*, and is the extra time it takes to do them perfectly worth the effort?

1. *Your housework.* Making beds; laundry (including folding of towels, sheets, and other items); setting tables; mopping; sweeping; cleaning

sinks, toilets, and tables; dusting; organizing; arranging shelves. Consider the frequency and level of perfection you expect in doing these chores.

2. *Your car.* Can you eat off the floor of your car? Are you allowed to eat *in* your car? How often and thoroughly do you clean and wash it? How closely do you follow recommended maintenance schedules (e.g., do you change oil *every* 3,000 miles or three months, whichever comes first)?

3. *Your grooming.* How much time do you spend looking "presentable" versus "perfect?" Can you *tell* the difference? Can others? On a daily basis: Do your shoes have to be so polished they could pass military inspection or your makeup so exactingly applied that it would do justice to a bride on her wedding day?

4. *Your work.* Do you spend too much time producing *perfect* work when you can gain all the benefits without significantly compromising your efforts by doing it *competently* instead?

5. *Your play.* Does every shot have to be *perfect* to give you pleasure? Are you always pushing yourself to do better, better, better? On a vacation do you have to relax *perfectly?*

I hope you are getting my drift here. Most of us suffer from perfectionitis in one or more parts of our lives. And the major problem with being perfect (versus competent) is the cost.

The cost *of perfection usually isn't worth it in terms of the time and hassle necessary to achieve it.*

HOW MANY TIMES HAVE YOU SEEN A HAPPY PERFECTIONIST?

Think of it this way: Imagine a perfectionist. What image do you see? Does this person look happy? Does it look like this person is *Romancing the Clock* and enjoying his or her time on Earth?

I think not. When I ask people to describe perfectionists I get adjectives such as "uptight," "anxious," "stressed," "never satisfied," "anal retentive," "picky," and "too demanding" (of themselves and others).

IF YOU'RE DEFUSING A NUCLEAR BOMB IN THE MIDDLE OF NEW YORK CITY, BE A PERFECTIONIST . . . OTHERWISE . . .

There are times when being a perfectionist is probably a good thing, as when human lives are at stake or the slightest error could mean the loss of millions of dollars of equipment. But in the vast majority of cases, both at home and at work, *competent* performance will suffice in place of *perfect* performance, and it will save you a great deal in terms of headaches, heartaches, hassles, and hours!

As my wife so aptly put it: "There is no such thing as a perfect man . . . all I ask is that you be a good one."

Hey, I can live with that . . . I hope you can, too.

Pursue a Healthy Lifestyle
It Enhances Joyful Living

Here's a brainteaser for you. Wendy Johnson is a dynamic, aggressive executive with a Fortune 500 company. For the past 15 years she's risen steadily through the corporate ranks, gaining respect and recognition in the business community. Yet, a few months short of her 45th birthday, Wendy Johnson suddenly loses her job. Why?

Because Wendy Johnson dropped dead—irrevocably cut down at the height of a promising career. Unusual? Unfortunately not. It has been estimated that the loss of production due to premature deaths costs American business in excess of $30 billion yearly, and that figure doesn't even start to approach the billions more lost through health-related absenteeism.

This chapter was adapted from M. Karlins, *The Human Use of Human Resources* (McGraw-Hill, 1981).

Yet, the real tragedy of Wendy Johnson goes beyond economic profit and loss—even beyond the personal loss of those who loved her. *The real tragedy of Wendy Johnson is that she died unnecessarily.* When a young woman like Wendy Johnson succumbs to a stroke or a coronary seizure, we are grimly reminded of our own mortality; yet in most cases it didn't have to happen (at least at such a young age). It was preventable. By making certain medically recommended changes in her personal behavior—*changes that in no way would have diminished her chances of succeeding in the business world*—Wendy Johnson could have dramatically increased her chances of living to full life expectancy, free from many of the medical problems that prematurely dull, cripple, and kill so many Americans.

LIVE LONGER, LIVE BETTER

Which brings me to you, who can still do something about your life. You don't have to go the way of a Wendy Johnson. Nobody, of course, can live forever, but medical science has given us new insights to greatly increase our chances for living full, alert, healthy lives. I will share these insights with you, but the effectiveness of what I have to say will depend on you and your willingness to implement the recommendations of medical science in your own life. As you read further, keep in mind what Dr. John Knowles, a president of the Rockefeller Foundation, said: "The next major advance in the health of the American people will result only from what the individual is willing to do for himself."

DOING BATTLE WITH EXCESSIVE STRESS

To help you help yourself toward better health, mental alertness, and longevity, medical science has identified many of the factors that can raise havoc with a person's health and well-being. None seems so culpable and widespread as stress. It has been called the "disease of our time"—the scourge of modern civilization.

Just what *is* stress? It is a condition we all experience. It can be caused by many things, such as frustrations, time binds, overwork, frightening experiences, emotional conflicts, and even pleasant events such as marriage or an outstanding personal achievement.

Please understand that normal amounts of stress never hurt anybody. In fact, moderate amounts of stress can actually enhance performance and make for a more meaningful, exciting life. Stress becomes dangerous only when it becomes *excessive*—forcing the body to function like a car with the accelerator stuck to the floor. When we become stressed, our bodies shift into a state of high physical arousal, preparing us for the so-called "fight-or-flight" response. If we experience this state too often, or stay in it too long, we will eventually break down like any overworked machine.

The word *stress* was borrowed from the language of physics and engineering, where it refers to a "force that tends to deform a body." How apt! That is *exactly* what excessive stress does to the human body in ugly, crippling ways. To compile a list of stress-related diseases is like thumbing through a medical dictionary. High blood pressure, heart attack, strokes, headaches, ulcers, allergies, infections, insomnia, asthma, diabetes, cancer, even accidents—all can be triggered and/or made more severe by excessive stress.

How do you know if you are under stress? One way is to visit your doctor for various tests: blood pressure, hormone levels, brain activity, and so forth. This is the preferred method, but it is not always possible on a day-to-day basis. However, as Dr. Hans Selye, the authority on stress, points out:

> There are other indices that anyone can judge. No two people react the same way, but the usual responses are . . . you will become more irritable and will sometimes suffer insomnia, even long after the stressor agent is gone. You will usually become less capable of concentrating, and you will have an increased desire to move about. I was talking with a businessman this morning who asked if he could walk back and forth because he couldn't think well sitting down. That is a stress symptom everyone will know.

Dr. Selye also points out that an increase in pulse rate and an increased tendency to sweat is common in persons undergoing stress.

DEVELOPING THE PROPER PSYCHOLOGICAL ATTITUDE TOWARD EXCESSIVE STRESS

Knowing when you are stressed is important, but it's only half the battle. It is also necessary to *do* something about it, and this is where the typical American confronts awesome difficulties. One of my close friends, a manager in a local business, put it bluntly: "Stress is as much a part of my life as my job and my family." Yet, many people are hesitant—even refuse—to reduce excessive stress in their own lives. Victimized by the stressful world they have helped create, they accept stress as a necessary component of existence. Stress becomes immutable, a force beyond the scope of change.

Then there are those who go so far as to extol the virtues of excessive stress, like the executive who, informed he had an ulcer, bragged, "I'm not concerned about it . . . don't you know that only successful people get ulcers?" It is these kinds of people, who see their stress-related miseries as "red badges of courage," proof of their worth, who are most unwilling to do anything about excessive stress in their lives. No wonder. They believe that being successful and undergoing excessive stress go hand in hand.

Unfortunately, they are wrong, and unless they change their attitude and their behavior, they may end up *dead* wrong.

To put it bluntly, there is no room for excessive stress in your life. If you want to *Romance the Clock*—if you want to love your time on Earth (and have enough *of* that time *to* love)—your main hope lies in keeping your own stress under control. I'll present you with some techniques to help you do this. But no techniques, however powerful, will work unless you have the proper psychological attitude toward stress in the first place. Thus, if you want to conquer excessive stress, you first must fully believe in the following three statements:

1. Excessive stress does *not* have to be an immutable force in your life. It can be overcome, and I'll show you how.

2. The quickest way to succumb to an enemy is to underestimate its strength. Learn to respect stress as a formidable opponent; realize what excessive stress can do to you; and decide you want to do something about it. Remember this statement: Excessive stress may be the single most powerful and pervasive enemy you face in achieving a healthy, joyous, and long life.

3. Realize that excessive stress does *not* improve your performance at work, at play, or anywhere. To the contrary, it has been shown to mentally and physically debilitate people—causing lapses in judgment, unnecessary effort, loss of concentration, reduction of creativity, interpersonal difficulties, and, in severe cases, nervous breakdowns, disease, and even death. You will *want* to overcome the "excessive stress oppressor" when you find that it dulls rather than sharpens your skills and performance.

Once you believe in and accept these three statements you've taken your first big step toward achieving a healthy life-style. You realize that excessive stress isn't good for you and you want to do something about it. Good. Now you're in the proper frame of mind to launch your own excessive-stress-reduction campaign and I'm going to give you a few stress-fighting weapons for your arsenal. These weapons, or stress-fighting techniques, can be used alone or in combination; but remember that each one, used conscientiously, can help turn the tide in your struggle against excessive stress. Try out the various weapons and choose the one(s) that work best for you.

THE RELAXATION RESPONSE

This excessive-stress weapon was popularized in a book of the same name, written by Dr. Herbert Benson with Miriam Klipper (New York: William Morrow, 1975). The material that follows was adapted from pp. 112–115 of that book.

The "relaxation response" seems so simple that many individuals dismiss it out of hand. Don't let its simplicity fool you—it works, and it works well. Furthermore, it is a weapon against stress that *all* of us possess, an innate gladiator waiting to do battle with excessive stress at our command.

In the words of Dr. Benson, "Each of us possesses a natural and innate protective mechanism against 'overstress,' which allows us to turn off harmful bodily effects, to counter the effects of the fight-or-flight response." The term Benson has attached to this protective mechanism is the "relaxation response," and he believes that by using it we can reduce the risk of stress-related illnesses such as heart attacks and related conditions—diseases that will cause the death of over 50 percent of the present population of the United States.

Just what *is* the relaxation response? Basically, it is a form of meditation. In calling forth the relaxation response, the meditator strives to achieve a state of restful alertness by spending two 20-minute periods each day in comfortable isolation, letting the mind empty of all thoughts and distractions.

By employing the relaxation response, a person reaps many physiological benefits: decreased oxygen consumption, diminished heart rate, lower respiratory rate, and increased skin resistance, which is inversely related to stress. The relaxation response has also been found to increase overall memory, reduce anxiety, decrease blood pressure in hypertensive individuals, heighten perceptual ability, relieve asthma, and even alleviate dependence on certain drugs, alcohol, and tobacco.

A real elixir, this relaxation response, your body's natural defense against the excessive stress spiral! Yet, as healthful as this technique is, many hard-nosed people shun it because it is a form of meditation: They see it as "faddish hocus-pocus." Well, here is the good news. You don't need a guru, a long flowing robe, or a mountain top to practice the relaxation response. You don't even need a special "mantra" given to you in some secret ceremony. All you need is 40 minutes a day and the willingness to follow the instructions of Dr. Benson.

1. Find a *quiet, calm environment* with as few distractions as possible. Sound, even background noise, may prevent elicitation of the response. Choose a convenient, suitable place—for example, at an office desk in a quiet room or a silent area of the house.

2. Choose a *mental device* to focus on—for example, a single-syllable sound or word. This sound or word is repeated silently or in a low, gentle tone. The purpose of the repetition is to free oneself from distracting thoughts by focusing solely on the sound or word, as repetition helps break the train of distracting thoughts. Many different words and sounds have been used in traditional practice. Because of its simplicity and neutrality, the word "*one*" is suggested.

3. Maintain a *passive attitude*. This is very important. The purpose of the relaxation response is to help you rest and relax, and this requires a completely passive attitude. When distracting thoughts occur, they are to be disregarded and attention redirected to the single-syllable sound or word. You should not worry about how well you are performing the technique, because this may prevent the relaxation response from occurring. Do not try to force the response, but adopt a let-it-happen attitude.

4. Meditate in a *comfortable position* (comfortable for you). You should sit in a comfortable chair in as restful a position as possible. Your goal is to reduce any undue muscular tension. The head may be supported; the arms should be balanced or supported as well. The shoes may be removed and feet propped up several inches, if desired. Loosen all tight-fitting clothes before beginning.

Observing Dr. Benson's four guidelines, you should be able to elicit your own relaxation response. Here is the way Dr. Benson suggests you actually conduct a session:

1. Sit quietly in a comfortable position.

2. Close your eyes.

3. Deeply relax all your muscles, beginning at your feet and progressing up to your face. Keep them relaxed.

4. Breathe through your nose (or mouth, if this is more comfortable). Become aware of your breathing. As you breathe out, say "One" silently to yourself. For example, breathe in . . . out, "One"; in . . . out, "One"; and so forth. Breathe easily and naturally.

5. Continue this practice for 20 minutes. You may open your eyes to check the time, but do not use an alarm. When you finish, sit quietly for several minutes, at first with your eyes closed and then with your eyes open. Do not stand up for a few minutes.

6. Remember not to worry about whether you are successfully achieving a deep level of relaxation. Maintain a passive attitude and permit relaxation to occur at its own pace. When distracting thoughts occur, try to ignore them by not dwelling upon them, and return to repeating "One." With practice the response should come with little effort. Practice the technique once or twice daily, but not within two hours after a meal, since the digestive processes seem to interfere with elicitation of the relaxation response.

There you have it. Your own innate weapon in the war on excessive stress. Use it wisely, and an equilibrium between tension and relaxation can be attained. "But," some of you may be worrying, "might the relaxation response upset my ability to stay 'sharp' and turn me into a zombie?"

To the contrary, the relaxation response will not only combat excessive stress but also enhance your alertness and performance. This seems particularly true at work, where testimonials to the value of the relaxation response are legion. Executives at many firms have called the relaxation response a "real battery charger"; "something that helped me concentrate properly for the first time in my life"; "a technique that helps me accomplish more with less work and effort." Dozens of American corporations, recognizing the value of the relaxation response, have initiated meditation programs at work—an idea Dr. Benson enthusiastically supports. He thinks employees should be given relaxation-response breaks instead of coffee breaks.

The next time you want to make a really great investment in 20 minutes, why don't you take a relaxation-response break? As you do, remember the words of psychologist Daniel Goleman: "Meditators become more relaxed the longer they have been at it. At the same time they become more alert, something other ways to relax fail to achieve because they do not train the ability to pay attention. The combination of relaxation and concentration allows us to do better at whatever we try."

EFFECTIVE EXERCISE

When I suggest that you practice the relaxation response, do not think I am recommending a less energetic existence—only a less stressful one. As a matter of fact, one of the best ways to beat the excessive stress syndrome is to live an active life, and our second stress-fighting weapon, exercise, will help you do just that.

"I don't know of a person who is highly regarded in medicine today who doesn't advocate exercise as an essential part of the life-style for healthful living." So observed C. Carson Conrad, as executive director of the President's Council on Physical Fitness. That observation was made way back in the 1970s! If you are willing to undertake an effective exercise program, you will probably find it the single most important contribution you can make to your job performance and good health.

The key word here is *effective*. To explain what I mean by effective, it is necessary to distinguish between two forms of exercise. One form, called *aerobics*, involves sustained physical activities that stimulate heart and lungs long enough to produce beneficial changes in the body. Such activities typically include walking briskly, jogging, swimming, cycling, and skipping rope. A second form of exercise does *not* require sustained action and includes sports such as bowling and baseball, plus body-building activities such as weightlifting and isometrics. These undertakings can be enjoyable, and some can give you an attractive physique, but they will *not* produce the health benefits of aerobic exercise. As science writer C. P. Gilmore notes:

Sports such as tennis and touch football may be strenuous but they generally call for intermittent rather than prolonged effort. Golf may be pleasant but it does not raise the pulse rate. Calisthenics make the muscles stronger and more flexible and help keep the joints limber, but are not usually indulged in vigorously enough or long enough. And, of course, the machines that jiggle and bounce the flesh may be fun, but they do nothing for the heart.

To put it bluntly, if you want to reap the health benefits from exercise, then you must be prepared to practice aerobics on a regular basis. This means that four to six days a week you need to spend time undertaking sustained, brisk physical activity.

Just *how* brisk? Actually, there has been some change of attitude in the scientific community since I first took up aerobics some 30 years ago. Back then I used to run between six and ten miles five times a week, in fact, running was seen as one of the ideal ways to gain the benefits of aerobic exercise. But current opinion suggests that exercise (like running) that is done *too* vigorously or too long might be unnecessary and can, in certain instances, even lead to bone and muscle injuries. Instead, it is recommended that a person who wants to gain the benefits of aerobic exercise can do so simply by walking briskly for 45 minutes a day, four to five times a week. What this means, best of all, is that the health benefits of aerobic fitness are within the reach of almost everyone, young and old. You don't need to be a young person or a "jock" to become aerobically fit—you don't even have to run. All you need is a little motivation, training, and perseverance, and you can walk your way to better health.

Just what *are* the benefits of regular, sustained, brisk exercise? One of the best ways to find out is to ask people involved in aerobics. Chances are their missionary zeal will send you scurrying for your sneakers. Most veteran exercisers agree that once you get into aerobics, you'll wonder how you ever got along without it. The benefits these people (including myself) have experienced first hand are documented by scientific research.

Would you be willing to spend some time, four to six days a week, to gain the advantages associated with lower blood pressure, substantial and permanent weight loss, healthier blood chemistry, and increased strength and efficiency of the heart? Regular aerobic exercise produces these beneficial physiological changes and more. It also helps those with diabetes and insomnia; many doctors believe it can aid in the battle against heart disease, the number one killer. Some medical authorities question the preventive value of sustained exercise but support the notion that it can be very useful in rehabilitating heart victims. Others, like the pioneering exercise authority Dr. Ken Cooper, believe that aerobics, properly followed, will lessen a person's chance of prematurely developing coronary heart disease or related vascular ailments.

Regular aerobic exercise has also improved the psychological well-being of many participants. A better self-image and more self-confidence are reported by many exercising business managers, along with increased alertness and ability to concentrate. These individuals report that they work with more energy and need less sleep when following an exercise regimen. A large study by the National Aeronautics and Space Administration showed that among NASA employees who closely followed a fitness program, more than 90 percent reported a feeling of better health and stamina, and about 50 percent said they had a more positive work attitude with less strain and tension.

This brings us to the last major benefit of aerobic exercise. It helps to reduce our major enemy: excessive stress. Simply put, exercise is a kind of pressure-release valve that provides an outlet for stored-up tensions and pent-up emotions. It allows us to express our aggressive drives in physical action rather than keep them bottled up inside where they can produce excessive stress effects. Also, a physically fit person's body is strengthened to a point where it can withstand excessive stress more effectively. As writers Walter McQuade and Ann Aikman have noted, "A person who is in good physical condition will withstand the assault of a virus, or a spell of overwork—or even a quarrel with the foreman—better than someone who isn't."

So much for the benefits of exercise. The human body wasn't built to sit still, so it shouldn't come as a surprise to discover that aerobic exercise is good for us. Yet some of you may be worrying about the possible *dangers* of sustained exercise; you may have heard stories about joggers dying or injuring themselves. Many of these stories turn out to be greatly exaggerated, but it is true that aerobic exercise does make some demands on the body and can be potentially dangerous for people who ignore simple, basic safety precautions. However, for those who *do* observe these precautions, sustained exercise is both safe and beneficial. In your own exercise program, observe these rules:

1. See your doctor for a complete medical examination *before* embarking on an exercise program. This is *very* important. The vast majority will be able to undertake aerobic exercise with no difficulty; however, a small number of people might have hidden problems, like an unknown heart condition, that could make sustained exercise risky. Tell your doctor you intend to begin an aerobic program, so that he or she can advise you of any possible problems. Most exercise physiologists recommend that the checkup include a cardio-pulmonary stress test.

2. Start slowly, and gradually work your way up to good aerobic fitness. If you've spent 30 years getting out of shape, don't expect youthful vigor to return as soon as you pull on your sweat socks!

3. Exercise regularly, at least three to four times a week, or do not exercise at all. If necessary, break your exercise sessions into smaller segments; for example, 10 minutes three times a day.

4. If you experience discomfort or pain while exercising, stop and check with your physician before you exercise again.

5. Before exercising, warm up and do some stretching to limber up and get your body toned for action. After finishing aerobic exercise it is recommended that you let your body readjust by doing some slow walking or a similar "cooling down" activity.

6. Do not overexert yourself during exercise. A good guideline for determining whether you exercise too vigorously is your pulse rate. Five minutes after you exercise it should be under 120, according to Dr. Cooper. Ten minutes after exercise it should be back to below 100. Dr. Cooper also suggests you watch for these symptoms of overexertion during exercise: "Tightness or pain in the chest, severe breathlessness, light-headedness, dizziness, loss of muscle control and nausea. Should you experience any of these symptoms," he cautions, "stop exercising immediately." From my own experience, I find that if you can't carry on a normal conversation with someone while exercising, you are probably overexerting yourself and need to scale back your exertion level.

There you have six rules for making *your* exercise program medically sound and worthwhile. Remember that you are exercising to achieve a healthier life-style. You defeat that purpose if you don't exercise safely.

The relaxation response and aerobic exercise are two weapons *all of us* can employ in the war on excessive stress. The next weapon I present is for combating a *specific* difficulty that creates excessive stress. If you don't have this difficulty, then you won't have to deploy this weapon against it. I hope you don't have to use it! Unfortunately, scientific evidence suggests that many adults do have this problem and should be doing something about it.

COMBATING TYPE A BEHAVIOR IN YOUR LIFE

The term *Type A behavior* was created by two heart specialists, Drs. Meyer Friedman and Ray Rosenman, to describe a behavior pattern they think is the major cause of premature coronary heart disease. They sound a very strong warning: "In the absence of Type A Behavior Pattern, coronary heart disease almost never occurs before seventy years of age . . . But when this behavior pattern is present, coronary heart disease can easily erupt in one's thirties or forties."

Just what *is* Type A behavior? Some describe it as "hurry sickness." Others label it "compulsive striving." Here is how Drs. Friedman and Rosenman define it:

. . . a style of living characterized by excesses or competitiveness, striving for achievement, aggressiveness (sometimes stringently repressed), time urgency, acceleration of common activities, restlessness, hostility, hyper-alertness, explosiveness of speech amplitude, tenseness of facial muscula-ture and feelings of struggle against the limitations of time and the insensitivity of the environment. This torrent of life is usually, but not always, channeled into a vocation or profession with such dedication that Type A persons often neglect other aspects of their life, such as family and recreation.

Sound familiar? I suspect it does. In our society, where racing against the clock is as American as apple pie, one should not be surprised at the number of Type A personalities around. The question is, "How *long* will they be around?" This is what worries Drs. Friedman and Rosenman, who suggest that people develop a *Type B* personality. In most ways, the Type B behavior pat-tern is the exact opposite of Type A. The Type B person isn't locked in a con-stant struggle to beat the clock. Such an individual can also be ambitious but feels more confident and secure than the Type A person and is able to be more relaxed. Most important, Type B individuals are just as successful as their Type A counterparts; they just handle themselves differently. They also are more likely to live long enough to enjoy the fruits of their labor.

To help determine what kind of personality *you* have, Type A or Type B, Friedman and Rosenman developed a Type A self-identification test. An adapted version from their book, *Type A Behavior and Your Heart* (Knopf, New York, 1974), is included here. Take a moment to read the instructions care-fully; then take the test. Be honest with yourself as you answer each item!

TYPE A SELF-IDENTIFICATION TEST

Instructions

Here is a test to help you determine whether you are a Type A or Type B personality. If you are honest in your self-appraisal . . . we believe you will not have too much trouble accomplishing this . . . Incidentally, we have found that Type A persons are by and large more common, and that if you are not quite sure about yourself, chances are that you, too, are Type A—not fully developed, perhaps, but bad enough to think about changing. And after you have assessed yourself, ask a friend or your spouse whether your self-assessment was accurate. If you disagree, your friend or spouse is probably right.

You Possess a Type A Behavior Pattern . . .

1. If you have (a) a habit of explosively accentuating various key words in your or-
   dinary speech even when there is no real need for such accentuation, and (b) a

tendency to utter the last few words of your sentences far more rapidly than the opening words.

2. If you *always* move, walk, and eat rapidly.

3. If you feel (particularly if you openly exhibit to others) an impatience with the rate at which most events take place. Here are some examples of this sort of impatience: if you become *unduly* irritated or even enraged when a car ahead of you in your lane runs at a pace you consider too slow; if you find it anguishing to wait in a line or to wait your turn to be seated at a restaurant; if you find it intolerable to watch others perform tasks you know you can do faster; if you find it difficult to restrain yourself from hurrying the speech of others.

4. If you indulge in *polyphasic* thought or performance, frequently striving to think of or do two or more things simultaneously. Some examples: While trying to listen to another person's speech you persist in continuing to think about an irrelevant subject; while golfing or fishing you continue to ponder your business or professional problems; while using an electric razor you also attempt to eat your breakfast or drive your car; while driving your car you attempt to dictate letters for your secretary. This is one of the commonest traits in the Type A person.

5. If you *always* find it difficult to refrain from talking about or bringing the theme of any conversation around to those subjects which especially interest and intrigue you, and when unable to accomplish this maneuver, you pretend to listen but really remain preoccupied with your own thoughts.

6. If you almost always feel vaguely guilty when you relax and do absolutely nothing for several hours or longer.

7. If you no longer observe the more important, interesting, or lovely objects that you encounter in your milieu. For example, if you enter a strange office, store, or home, and after leaving any of these places you cannot recall what was in them, you no longer are observing well—or for that matter enjoying life very much.

8. If you do not have any time to spare to become the things worth *being* because you are so preoccupied with getting the things worth *having*.

9. If you attempt to schedule more and more in less and less time, and in doing so make fewer and fewer allowances for unforeseen contingencies. A concomitant of this is a *chronic sense of time urgency*, one of the core components of the Type A behavior pattern.

10. If on meeting another severely afflicted Type A person, instead of feeling compassion for his affliction, you find yourself compelled to "challenge" him. This is a telltale trait because no one arouses the aggressive and/or hostile feelings of one Type A subject more quickly than another Type A subject.

11. If you resort to certain characteristic gestures or nervous tics. For example, if in conversation you frequently clench your fist, or bang your hand upon a table, or pound one fist into the palm of your other hand in order to emphasize a conversational point, you are exhibiting Type A gestures. Similarly, if the corners of your mouth spasmodically, in ticlike fashion, jerk backward slightly, exposing your teeth, or if you habitually clench your jaw, or even grind your teeth, you are subject to muscular phenomena suggesting the presence of a continuous *struggle*, which is, of course, the kernel of the Type A behavior pattern.

12. If you believe that whatever success you have enjoyed has been due in good part to your ability to get things done faster than other people, and if you are afraid to stop doing everything faster and faster.

13. If you find yourself increasingly and ineluctably committed to translating and evaluating not only your own but also the activities of others in terms of numbers.

You Possess the Type B Behavior Pattern . . .

1. If you are completely free of *all* the habits and exhibit none of the traits shown by the severely afflicted Type A person.

2. If you never suffer from a sense of time urgency with its accompanying impatience.

3. If you harbor no free-floating hostility, and you feel no need to display or discuss either your achievements or accomplishments unless such exposure is demanded by the situation.

4. If, when you play, you do so to find fun and relaxation, not to exhibit your superiority at any cost.

5. If you can relax without guilt, just as you can work without agitation.

How did you do? Of course, nobody is a pure Type A or Type B person—but, in general, which behavior pattern seems to fit you best? If you possess many of the characteristics of the Type A personality, you should take steps *now* to try and do something about it. As Friedman and Rosenman point out, ". . . in the majority of cases, Type A Behavior Patterns can be altered and altered drastically; and it is a terribly dangerous delusion to believe otherwise."

Regretfully, there is no simple formula that can transform you from a Type A into a Type B personality overnight. Changing behavior patterns, particularly ones as socially acceptable and deeply ingrained as Type A behavior patterns, will take a lot of time and conscientious effort. In extreme cases, moving away from destructive Type A behavior will require significant changes in your basic life-style. But the changes *can* be made, and they *will* be worth making! To help you, Friedman and Rosenman offer some good suggestions. Here are a few of them, along with some of my own.

1. Realize that you can be just as successful in business by being Type B as by being Type A. Friedman and Rosenman see Type A behavior as actually *detrimental* to long-term success, and they inform Type A business people: "If you have been successful, it is not *because* of your Type A Behavior Pattern, but *despite* it."

2. Do not think you'll be lucky enough to escape the medical consequences of long-term Type A behavior. Many Type A persons delude themselves about this, and therefore don't try to modify their potentially dangerous actions.

3. During each day, set some time aside for rest and relaxation.

4. Allow yourself enough time to get things done, so that you won't have to feel pressured and rushed. For example, leave ample time between your appointments.

5. Quit trying to think of or do more than one thing at a time. Concentrate on one task at a time.

6. Live by the calendar, not the stopwatch.

7. Learn to take breaks when doing work that causes stress.

8. Try to work in a setting that promotes peace of mind. Constant interruptions, messy desks, and drab surroundings do not help soothe the ragged mind.

9. Remind yourself once a day that no enterprise ever failed because it was executed too slowly, too well.

10. Acquire a taste for reading.

11. Spend some time by yourself.

12. When facing a task, ask yourself two questions: Will this matter be important 5 years from now? Must I do this right now, or do I have enough time to think about the *best* way to accomplish it.

13. Don't think you have to finish all your work by 5 P.M. every day. The world will still be around when you wake up the next morning.

14. Avoid irritating, overcompetitive people.

15. Learn to slow down and be patient with the rate at which events take place. When you act rushed, you will feel pressured. Eat slower; walk

slower; don't drive as if you were in the Indianapolis 500; try to talk slower; quit rushing the conversation of others; learn to wait in line without getting the jitters.

I hope you will find these 15 suggestions helpful in battling Type A behavior in *your* life. The book *Type A Behavior And Your Heart* by Friedman and Rosenman offers these and additional suggestions if you would like further methods for combating the Type A syndrome. The two doctors also emphasize that it's never too late to begin a Type A prevention program—even if you're in your sixties and a victim of one or more heart attacks. One doctor began just such a program after a heart attack of his own. His name is Meyer Friedman.

A FINAL WEAPON IN YOUR BATTLE FOR A HEALTHY LIFE-STYLE

The relaxation response. Exercise. Overcoming Type A behavior—three ways you can enhance joyful living and increase the probability you will experience a longer life at the same time! And there's a fourth and final weapon as well: *moderation*.

After decades of scientific research and anecdotal evidence, it is clear that *excess* is the enemy of psychobiological well-being, and *moderation* is its ally. At first glance, a life of moderation might sound boring, but this need not be the case. Moderate amounts of food and drink, moderate amounts of exercise, moderation in the way we "let it all hang out" and have fun—all this can be satisfying without being excessive. Living in the fast lane leads to breakdowns and a dulling of the senses.

The human body was not meant to remain in high gear hour after hour, day after day. A life of excess creates excessive stress, which, as we have learned, is anathema to a healthy life-style.

Moderation in the way we live is not a prescription for tedium; rather, it is a strategy for living longer, stronger, and more successfully, at home, at work, and in all the things we do. Moderation is the mark of a wise person, a person who has learned the best way to love his or her time on Earth.

Use moderation as a weapon to effectively battle excessive stress. It's worth the effort!

THE BOTTOM LINE

Heart attacks, excessive stress, relaxation, exercise, moderation—I've deluged you with a lot of information; tendered some suggestions; sounded some warnings; and, I hope, sparked your enthusiasm for practicing a healthy life-style in the pursuit of joyful living.

Social historians tell us we are living in an age of ecological awareness. We speak of the need to reduce waste, to save precious resources. Do you know of any greater waste than the needless waste of human life? Do you know of any resource more precious than the human resource? Practice a little *personal* ecology; take the steps necessary to enhance your chances for a healthier, happier, and more productive life.

You're worth it.

When You Must Do Battle . . . Pick Your Fights with Care

It's hard to *Romance the Clock* when, as the old saying goes, someone is try-ing to "clean" yours! Interpersonal conflicts account for some of the most unpleasant and wasted periods of time in our lives. In an ideal world there would be no need for this chapter. Sadly, we're not living on that planet! So, this Action Step gives us the next best option: *learning how to deal with inter-personal conflict in a manner that minimizes the hassles and time you'll need to spend in this negative activity.* In accomplishing this objective we will be ex-amining four principles of effective interpersonal conflict control: (1) Don't fight battles you have little or no chance of winning; (2) Don't engage in battles not worth the fight; (3) Don't win battles that will cost you the war; and (4) Don't rule out retreat as an eventual path to victory.

En garde!

DON'T FIGHT BATTLES YOU HAVE LITTLE OR NO CHANCE OF WINNING

Don't you just love an underdog? I mean, you gotta feel good about that David and Goliath match-up. But there can be danger in this kind of affection if we see it as a model for what we can accomplish in battles where we're prohibitive underdogs.

The reason why people like David are remembered is because they prove the exception to the rule. They are news because they were victorious in battles they never should have won. To use them as role models in your approach to conflict—to imagine you can duplicate their success in battles you literally have no chance of winning—is a risky strategy that almost always leads to frustration and failure.

I am not saying you should avoid fighting battles where there is a chance you might lose. I'm not even saying to keep out of battles where it's more *likely* you'll lose than win. Sometimes such battles are worth the long odds you face because you stand to benefit greatly if you should emerge victorious. What I *am* saying is to stay away from battles where you are a *prohibitive underdog* to win—where it would literally take a miracle (David was well-connected, after all) to come out on top.

But how do you *know* what your chances are for victory or defeat? Sometimes you won't, but usually past experience and common sense will give you a pretty good estimate of whether you will succeed or fail in your mission. It is important that you make an honest appraisal of your chances to win or lose any battle *before* you decide to take it on or avoid it. Those people whom I like to refer to as "underdog Pollyannas" usually *overestimate* their chances of winning and thus engage in battles they have no business fighting!

I see these people everywhere, modern-day Don Quixotes tilting at their designated windmills, spending hour after frustrating hour in fruitless combat. Some of these hapless warriors will spend literally years battling people they cannot change, rules they cannot repeal, and/or organizations they cannot beat. And here's the saddest part: The harder they fight, the more the experience eats at them, consumes them, makes their lives miserable. When they finally lose the battle, as they most surely will, their sense of frustration and rage can linger on for months, even years. That's certainly no way to *Romance the Clock* and love your life on Earth!

Don't waste your time, energy and emotion fighting battles you have little or no chance of winning! It's a drain on your time and spirit you can ill afford. One classic example of this kind of fruitless struggle is often seen in marriages in which one spouse, say the wife, decides she can "change" her husband into the kind of man she desires. The fact that her mate has made it clear through his behavior, his comments, and his courtship that he has no intention of changing doesn't dampen the enthusiasm or persistence of his spouse who believes otherwise. The end result? Unhappiness in both partners, interpersonal frustration and tension, and, in many cases, disillusionment and eventual divorce.

"But wait a minute," you say. "What about people who fight battles they know they will lose because to do otherwise would be *morally* wrong?"

My answer to this question is: If you truly believe that what you are fighting for is so morally important that you are willing to lose for the principle involved, by all means fight on! But be honest with yourself when you use this line of reasoning to justify fighting battles you have little or no chance of winning. On careful reflection you might discover you are using moral justifications to do battle when, in fact, morality might just be a side (or bogus) issue and the *real* reason(s) for your involvement might be totally different.

The next time you think about doing battle against some perceived injustice or undesirable state of affairs it might be wise to pause a moment and consider a prayer that is used by Alcoholics Anonymous. It is called the *Serenity Prayer*, and it speaks volumes on the issue of fighting battles you have little or no chance of winning.

> God, grant me the serenity
> To accept the things I cannot change,
> Courage to change the things I can,
> And wisdom to know the difference.

I hope such serenity and wisdom will be yours.

DON'T ENGAGE IN BATTLES NOT WORTH THE FIGHT

How many times has this happened to you? You're in a bit of a rush. You pull into a nearby convenience store with gas pumps outside and put $18 worth of fuel into your car. After you finish, you go inside to pay. You use your credit card. The clerk punches up the sale and hands you the slip for your signature. You sign and he hands you a duplicate copy. You don't check the receipt, you just jam it in your pocket and hurry on your way.

Sound familiar? It should. I know hardly anyone who checks their receipts every time they get one

Now, let's assume it's a month later. You get your credit card statement and you notice that something is wrong. The convenience store where you had stopped for gas shows a charge for $48! Impossible, you reason, you're certain you only purchased $18 worth of gas.

After an extensive search, you are lucky enough to find the gas receipt. Now you'll have the proof you need to substantiate your $18 purchase. You are guessing that the credit card company must have mistakenly punched in a "4" where the "1" should have gone. You're half right: The "four" is there—but it's on the receipt! A receipt *you* signed for $48 worth of gas.

You call the credit card company to complain. You explain that there is no way your tank could hold $48 worth of gas and that the clerk must have entered the wrong numbers.

The customer satisfaction representative pulls up your account on the screen and looks at the charge. "Did you sign the slip?" he asks.

"Yes, but what does that have to do with it?"

"Once you sign the receipt it is a legal sale. Possibly you purchased something else that brought the total to $48."

You assure the representative that didn't happen. You can't, however, explain away the fact that you signed the receipt. Your excuse that "no one looks at those things before they sign them, anyway," doesn't sway the credit card representative. He announces his verdict: "You'll have to go to the merchant and have them put in a credit for the amount you claim you were incorrectly billed."

You're mad. You've spent a half hour searching for the receipt and another half hour on the phone. One hour and you're still out $30.

The next day you go 10 miles out of your way to visit the convenience store and get the $30 credited back to your account. The clerk looks at the receipt, nods sympathetically, and says she can't do a thing. Only a manager can make that kind of adjustment. "And where is the manager?" you ask.

"Gone to lunch," explains the clerk.

Not wanting to wait an hour, you leave in a huff. You return the following week. This time the manager is there and she listens to your story.

"If the figure was wrong, why did you sign the charge slip?" she wanted to know.

You don't appreciate the tone of her voice *or* the question. The conversation gets a bit testy, but in the end the woman says she'll take care of it. "I need a copy of the receipt," she adds.

You don't have a copy.

"Can't do it without a copy," she warns.

You expend 15 furious minutes driving around to locate a copy machine. It costs you a dime to make a duplicate. You're now out $30.10, plus the cost of gas driving to and from the convenience store and the copy center.

You return to the convenience store and hand the manager the copy of the receipt. You have now spent a total of almost three hours and a lot of anger on this reimbursement.

Your credit card statement comes the next month. Guess what? The charge hasn't been adjusted. You call the credit card company. They say they haven't received the credit from the merchant. You call the convenience store. After several attempts you get the manager on the phone. She claims the money was credited back to your account.

Arguments continue in a massive game of telephone triangle: you, the convenience store manager, and the credit card company representative.

To cut a very long story short: After more than six hours of hassle, heartburn, and headaches, the misappropriated $30 is recredited to your account.

Now, I ask you: *Was the battle worth it?*

Well, according to Tim Harris, the Detroit businessman who experienced this nightmare, the answer is a definite NO! "Not for the principal *or* the principle," was the way he put it. "I could have made more money working at a minimum wage job," he lamented, "and not had to endure all the anger and frustration the credit card fiasco caused me."

Look back in your own life (you probably won't have to go very far). Have you engaged in battles not worth the fight? Maybe it was a fight with your spouse. (You can usually tell if the battle wasn't worth it if you can't remember what caused the fight in the first place!) Perhaps it was over a minor indiscretion or an inadvertent snub. Maybe it was over money or some other possession. Whatever it was, ask yourself: *Was the battle worth it . . . win or lose?*

There are two basic reasons for not engaging in battles not worth the fight:

1. *The battle ends up costing more (in terms of time, aggravation, and stress) than what it was fought for!* Kind of like a person spending $20 on a carnival sideshow game to win a 50-cent doll. (At least the person at the sideshow game was probably having fun, which is more than one can say for a person in the midst of a battle not worth fighting.)

2. *The battle can expand beyond its initial objective.* Even though it might begin over a minor issue, a battle can grow into a full-fledged war. Like a minor brush fire that becomes a major forest fire, there is always the danger that any fight can go beyond the original problem and get far nastier and more severe than warranted by the initial issues. This happened recently in Los Angeles. Two drivers involved in a minor fender-bender got out of their cars and began to argue. Things escalated, and in a matter of minutes one of the combatants went back to his car, got out a gun, and shot the other driver dead.

***

The next time someone says something to you that causes offense, pause for a moment and ask yourself: "Is this worth getting in a fight over . . . even if I win?

***

The next time someone makes a mistake that costs you money and/or aggravation, pause for a moment and ask yourself: "Is this worth getting in a fight over . . . even if I win?

***

The next time someone challenges you to do battle, pause for a moment and ask yourself: "Is this worth getting in a fight over . . . even if I win?

***

If you aren't sure, or the answer is "no," then I say: Avoid the battle. Save yourself the hurt and hassle. And remember, if you do choose to enter the fray, you might *not* win. You *could* lose!

DON'T WIN BATTLES THAT WILL COST YOU THE WAR

This is a true story, I kid you not! Back when I was a graduate student at Princeton University, people used to claim it was easier to graduate than to get a parking space for your car. I assumed they were joking, but parking *was* a problem. There were very few spaces, and most of those were reserved for faculty. So I hope you can appreciate my excitement when I got my *own* special parking space. It was assigned to me when I got a faculty appointment after completing my Ph.D. It was a great spot, too, right behind my office in the psychology building.

I remember arriving for the first day of class 10 minutes early, just so I could drive into my reserved spot and sit joyfully in parked splendor. There I serenely watched as less fortunate individuals desperately circled the lot in search of a space. I had been there and done that—but never again! I waxed poetic:

> The world it was a perfect place
> When I got my private parking space!

My first year on the faculty was great: great students, great research, great parking. My contract was renewed for a second year, and all things grand and glorious continued to occur.

Until that fateful day in October.

It was a day of parking lot pathos. I had just turned into the psychology building parking lot when I saw a most unsettling sight: Directly in front of me, parked brazenly in *my* reserved spot, was the experimental psychologist's *Ratmobile*. This was actually a motor home that had been converted into a mobile rat lab, complete with furry rodents in cages, experimental apparatus, and demonstration equipment.

The fact that I was a social psychologist made this intrusion into my parking place particularly annoying. As long as I had been at Princeton there had been no love lost between us social psychologists and the experimental psychologists who ran the Ratmobile. Thus, this territorial invasion had all the impact of insult added to injury.

I lost no time protesting the parking violation directly to the department chairman. I told him I hoped the parking violation was an unfortunate accident that would be rectified immediately.

It wasn't.

"The mobile rat lab is going to have to stay there," the chairman informed me. "There was no other place for it."

I should have guessed he'd demonstrate such insensitivity. He was a *rat man* himself.

"What about my faculty parking rights?" I asked.

"Parking *privilege*," the chairman corrected. "You are the faculty member with least seniority, so you were the one who lost your spot."

"And that's it?" I said, an edge of disbelief in my voice. "There's nothing I can do about it?"

"Well," the chairman said jauntily, "you can appeal the decision to the university president, I guess."

He was kidding.

I wasn't.

I was furious. I called the president's office that very afternoon. When the secretary answered, I identified myself as Dr. Karlins, a faculty member, and said I needed to speak with the president about a problem. When the secretary asked the nature of the problem I told her it was "personal."

I got an appointment the following week. That gave me eight days to stew over the issue, my anger growing each day as I saw the Ratmobile comfortably resting in *my* parking spot while I had to walk three blocks to work.

When the day of the appointment finally arrived I was *ready!* I entered the president's reception area five minutes early and identified myself to the woman sitting at a desk just inside the door.

As soon as she heard my name the woman said: "Go right in, the president is expecting you." She motioned toward a door a few feet behind her desk.

I thanked her, walked to the door, opened it, and stepped into a huge room. Directly in front of me, in a glass case, was the University Mace, an impressive looking scepter that was used in various ceremonial events and processions. Beyond the case, the president sat at an ornate wooden desk. He was in a leather swivel chair that he turned slightly to face me when I entered. He was smoking a pipe and looking very regal. For a moment I wondered if this was really such a great idea, and then the vision of the Ratmobile pushed all doubts from my mind.

"You're Dr. Karlins," the president said.

"Yes, sir," I answered respectfully. "Thanks for taking the time to see me."

"That's fine." The president studied me for several moments before saying anything further. I watched the smoke rising from his pipe, drifting upward in a thin column between his eyes and spreading outward toward the ceiling. "My secretary said you were having a *personal* problem. Is that correct?"

"Yes, sir."

"What *kind* of problem?" The president looked directly at me as he asked the question.

"A parking problem," I replied.

If the president of Princeton University felt any amazement or anger that a lowly faculty instructor would take up his valuable time with a *parking* problem, he never let it show. His expression never changed. His gaze never wavered. Still looking at me, he said, "What *type* of problem would that be?"

I told him the whole story. I explained my initial pride over receiving the parking space, how much it meant to me, and my horror when I found it taken over by the territory-grabbing experimental psychologists and their *Ratmobile*. I told him I thought the chairman was in collusion with the "rat men," too.

The president listened attentively as I described my predicament. When I finished, he took the pipe from his mouth and studied it for a few moments. Then he returned his attention to me.

"Tell you what," he said in a measured voice. "Today is Tuesday. Next Monday you check back at the parking lot and see if your space is available."

"And if it isn't . . ." I asked cautiously.

"Just check it on Monday," the president repeated and rose from his chair.

It was obvious the meeting was at an end.

The rest of the week was a wash-out for work or anything else. All I could think about was Monday.

When the day finally came I woke early, dressed and ate quickly, and arrived at the psychology building 15 minutes early. As I turned into the driveway I said a silent prayer and directed my attention to the parking space. It was *Empty!* Gloriously, totally unoccupied.

I eased my way into the space and sat there in total triumph, savoring my victory. I had won the battle! The Ratmobile was gone, banished from *my* space.

Later that year it came time for contract renewals. Faculty appointments for the following year were being made.

Guess what: My contract wasn't renewed. I was *out* of there! *Persona non grata.*

I had won the parking battle and lost the employment war.

> ### Don't win battles that will cost you the war.

It was a lesson I will never forget, and I hope you won't, either.

Whenever you confront a problem that could lead to a battle, always take a "big picture" view of the situation. Consider the impact of your decision to do battle in a long-term perspective, always considering any possible long-term consequences of your actions. The feelings of elation that come with a battle won are far too costly if that momentary victory leads to total defeat further down the road!

DON'T RULE OUT RETREAT AS AN EVENTUAL PATH TO VICTORY

At the university where I currently teach, all students are required to receive a test grade in the first five weeks of the course so they will know how they're performing before the "drop" deadline. The "drop" deadline is the last day the student can withdraw from the course without penalty. With this grade information, it is assumed that students can make an informed decision as to the advisability of staying in the course.

Some can't. They want my advice. They come into my office, some with scores so low they even missed the *sample* question! They want me to tell them if they should stay in the course or drop it.

I ask the students *why* they think they received such a low score. If they come up with a reason that suggests they can improve their score on the next test (for instance, they didn't study for the test or they were sick on the day they took it), then I will sometimes recommend they stick it out.

On the other hand, if the failing students have studied hard for the test and there is no good reason to assume they will do much better on the next one, then I suggest they drop the course and take it at a later time (if at all) when they are better prepared to achieve higher scores.

Often these students reject my advice and say they don't want to drop the course. When I ask why, their answers convey the same basic message: "I want to stay in the course because I'm not a quitter." These students feel that once they've started the course it would be wrong to give up, even in the face of almost certain failure.

Perhaps these students are related to General Custer.

Perseverance, not being a quitter, and staying the course are admirable qualities in a person. However, such qualities can become dysfunctional when not tempered with the flexibility that allows an individual to recognize that retreat is not disgraceful or cowardly, but a viable option that allows a person to back off, regroup, and return to the battle at a later time when the chances for victory have improved.

To lose the battle simply because you don't want to retreat is a serious error in strategy and a terrible waste of resources.

Why is it so hard for people who are normally logical, reasonable, level-headed thinkers to consider retreat as a viable way to cut losses and enhance chances for success down the road?

The first reason is *ego*. It is hard to admit that you are in over your head. It is difficult to swallow your pride and withdraw, even if that withdrawal is only temporary. Better to go out in a blaze of glory! Well, that might be the Hollywood answer to retreat; but it certainly shouldn't be yours.

The second reason is *inertia*. Once you're headed in a specific direction, even if it's the wrong one, the tendency is to maintain that direction.

The third reason is *resources already invested*. When you've already put a lot of time, effort, and/or money into a project or activity it is hard to give it up by pulling back. I see this all the time with gamblers in places like Las Vegas. They lose their limit at the table but, rather than beating a hasty and sensible retreat, they press on, digging into their pockets and shoving more money into play. Gamblers with self-control have a saying about refusing to retreat in the face of mounting losses: "Don't throw good money after bad." (Or, as Kenny Rogers used to sing: "You have to know when to hold 'em and know when to fold 'em.") In other words, cut your losses and return at a later time when your luck and/or skill might be at a higher level, giving you a better chance of victory.

Sometimes, when we are willing to retreat from a battle that is going badly, it gives us the opportunity to reassess the situation from a cooler, more objective view. It is then that we might come to realize that the battle is no longer worth fighting, either because we have no realistic chance of winning in the long run or we were defending an untenable position in the the first place. Then we can refrain from contesting that particular battle any further and preserve what resources we have left for other engagements that provide a better chance for victory.

A case in point: A colleague of mine was writing a book. He finished 150 pages and sent them to the editor. The editor wrote back that he felt the book was heading in the wrong direction and that the author might want to start again from a different angle. My colleague resisted the suggestion. Why? By his own admission it was because "I have too much invested in this approach to change it." After struggling through another 50 pages, he finally realized that further effort was futile; he was, in the gambling analogy, simply throwing "good words after bad!" So he retreated, regrouped, and returned to the compositional battlefield. He started at page one and used a different approach. The result? A successful manuscript.

RETREAT, REGROUP, RETURN!

Do you remember the words of General MacArthur when he retreated from the Philippines during the Second World War? He said: "I shall return." And he did. Victoriously.

The sooner you are able to cut off nonproductive efforts, the greater will be your savings in terms of time, effort, and resources. It is foolish and fruitless to increase the immensity of your defeat just because of ego, inertia, and/or resources already invested. Retreat, used as a tactical approach in battle, is not defeat. It is a way to buy time, change tactics, or develop the necessary skills and resources to increase the chances of victory at a later time.

Retreat, regroup, return! Custer didn't do it. MacArthur did. You can, too.

When it comes to *Romancing the Clock* effectively, you must learn to become a *Time Commander* in dealing with any battles you face:

> 1. **Don't fight battles you have little or no chance of winning.**
> 2. **Don't engage in battles not worth the fight.**
> 3. **Don't win battles that will cost you the war.**
> 4. **Don't rule out retreat as an eventual path to victory.**

These are the four basic principles that will help you enhance the positive aspects of your life and reduce the hassles and unpleasantries that are an ever-present threat to your well-being.

Conflicts will always be a part of life. Handle them as a *Time Commander* and you will be doing all you can to help *love your time on Earth.*

A Metaphor to Live By

A story is told of a man who sets off to find enlightenment. He goes to China in search of an old Master who lives high in the Zenfu Mountains. It is said of this Master that he is an individual of great wisdom and gentle nature. When the man finally reaches the Master's simple shelter, set atop the highest mountain peak in the region, the Wise One is sitting on a large, flat boulder gazing out toward the horizon. The man approaches quietly, reverently—not wanting to disturb the old man's meditation. Without turning or altering his gaze, the Master acknowledges the presence of his guest.

"What is it you seek?" he asks in a voice just a whisper above the wind.

The man climbs upon the rock and sits down next to the Master. "I wish to know the secret of time: how to *use* it to find happiness and lose sadness in my life."

The Master reaches down beside him, picks up a well-worn book, and hands it to his visitor. "This book holds all the answers to the question you have asked."

The man accepts the book gratefully. "You'd give this to me?" he asks, a touch of awe in his voice.

The Master shakes his head sadly. "No, my son, this is my only copy. You'll need to get yours off the Internet or from a bookstore."

The man notes the title of the book: *Romancing the Clock*. "Interesting title," he acknowledges. "But since I've come all this way, could you at least summarize the lesson it teaches?"

"It teaches a most simple truth," the Master replies. "An obvious truth. Yet, it is the simplest, most obvious truths that are often the most profound." A wisp of a smile plays upon the old man's face. "I will summarize for you the lesson the book teaches, but first you must solve this riddle: Why is it that the simplest, most obvious truths are the ones that most often elude us—that remain invisible to us though totally in our sight?"

The man ponders the riddle without finding an answer. "Beats the hell out of me," he admits, forgetting for a moment that he is on top of a mountain sitting next to an Enlightened One. "Sorry about that," he says sheepishly. "I get angry when I can't answer questions, and I never was much good at riddles."

"Do not feel bad," the Master commiserates, "I've been up here for 30 years trying to find the answer myself."

"Yet you persist," the man says respectfully.

"I have no choice," the Master responds glumly. "My doctoral committee at Berkeley won't award me my degree until I solve the riddle."

"How can you afford the tuition costs for so long?" the man marvels, noting the lack of material goods anywhere on the mountain peak.

"This is getting off the subject," the Master cautions, taking a deep breath and letting it flow slowly from his body. "You have asked for the simple truth that summarizes the lessons of the book."

"Yes." The man leans closer to the Master to hear his words.

"Look out from where we sit . . . what do you see?"

"What does that have to do with the summary?" the man inquires.

"This is the way Enlightened Ones impart knowledge," the Master explains.

"Oh." The man scans the scene before him. "I see two mountains off in the distance with a valley running between them."

"Yes," the Master agrees. "Those are *physical* mountains you can see. Now imagine that you are standing in the valley between two mountains, your own *personal* mountains.

The man closes his eyes and imagines.

"And imagine further that one mountain represents all the *positive* things in your life and the other mountain represents all the *negative* things or *hassles* in your life."

The man imagines further.

"Finally, imagine that you hold a shovel in your hands."

"I got it," the man says, locking the image in his mind.

"The way to find happiness and lose sadness is to increase the size of the positive mountain and reduce the size of the negative mountain in your life."

"And that is done how . . . ?"

"Many ways, my son. Just as the physical mountains you saw before you were shaped from the forces of nature in the past so, too, have your personal mountains been shaped by what happened to you and what you have done in the past. If you want to change those mountains now, it will be your current and future actions that will reshape them."

The man contemplated what he had just heard. He liked it when the Master called him "son" but wondered if "grasshopper" might be more complimentary. "But how do I reshape them?" he wondered aloud.

"That is where the shovel comes in," the Master explained. "It symbolizes actions you can take to change your personal mountains. You can use your shovel to chip away at the negative mountain whenever you can, to reduce its size by shoveling away the negatives in your life.

"And the positive mountain . . .?"

"Use your shovel to dig up the positive experiences in the valley around you and add them to the positive mountain to increase its size. *Increase* the positive mountain and *decrease* the negative mountain. This is the key to loving your time on Earth."

The man remained silent for several minutes, considering what the Master had told him. "This is the lesson the book teaches?"

The Master nodded affirmatively. "It is. In *Star Trek* terminology it would be called the *Prime Directive*: "Accentuate the positives and reduce the negatives in your life." The book tells you how to do it.

Accentuate the positives and reduce the negatives in your life.

The man repeated the words slowly, imagining himself digging away at the negative mountain and adding to the positive one. It was a metaphor he could understand . . . and a program he could undertake. All he needed to know was "how" to proceed with his geographical reconfiguration, and the book recommended by the Master would tell him how.

The man was grateful for the wisdom the Master had shared with him and offered his heartfelt thanks.

The master acknowledged the gesture and bade him farewell.

Easing himself off his rocky perch, the man prepared to take the first steps of his long journey down the mountain. He looked up at the Master one last time to say goodbye. But this time the Master did not respond. The Enlightened One was blinded to all but the movement of a cloud as it floated freely, a singular white dot against the deep blue backdrop of God's perfect sky.

Exercises and Applications
Introduction

This new section of the book was created in response to reader feedback from the first edition of *Romancing the Clock*. Additional self-administered exercises—like the *Aspiration–Occupation Exercise* in Chapter 6—are included in the second edition to help readers more successfully apply what they are learning in their everyday lives. The exercises that follow are designed to do just that: to assist you in translating knowledge into action . . . taking the time-management principles I have described and using them to live a more joyful, meaningful life.

Romancing the Clock is not a passive activity. It requires an active, committed pursuit of the lifestyle I describe in the book. These exercises also require your *active* participation. The more thought and energy you put into completing the tasks, the more benefits you will gain from your efforts. Remember the wisdom captured in the computer programmer's motto: "Garbage in, garbage out." If you tackle these exercises with enthusiasm and commitment, you will gain a better understanding of yourself and what you need to do to live your life to the fullest. However, if you complete the exercises in a perfunctory manner, investing very little of yourself in completing the tasks . . . then don't expect to accrue significant dividends from your efforts.

As you complete the various exercises and applications, don't forget that as growing and developing human beings we change over time; therefore, some of the responses you make today won't be reflective of the way you are—or what you want—1, 5, 10, or even 20 years down the road. For this reason, it might be instructive and helpful if you revisit these exercises at reasonable intervals in the years to come; that way, you can assess over time if you are still on the right course for living joyfully or, if not, what "midcourse" corrections you need to make in your life's journey.

Introductory Exercise

IMPROVING YOUR HOURGLASS FIGURE

PURPOSES OF THIS EXERCISE

1. To stimulate your thinking about time management: What kind of time management problems exist, and what you might do to overcome them.

2. If you have already read the book (ignore this question if you have not yet read the text): To ascertain how well you have learned the material in *Romancing the Clock*.

INSTRUCTIONS

Diane and Steve Williams are a two-career couple (accountant and human resource manager, respectively) who each work approximately 50 hours per week, spending the rest of their time with their friends and young daughter, Heather, who is 3 years old. They are not wealthy, but they are able to afford a four-bedroom home and have some discretionary income to spend each month. On this particular Sunday evening, they are sitting in their family room lamenting the lack of time in their lives—a frequently discussed topic. The following is a transcript of their conversation. **When you have finished reading the conversation, answer these two questions: (1) What time management mistakes did Diane and/or Steve make? (Use their comments to identify their mistakes.) (2) What advice might you give to help them become better time managers? Please record your answers in the space provided at the end of the conversation transcript.**

Diane: Last night Gayle called about meeting for lunch. I had to say "no." There's never enough hours in the day. I swear . . . I just don't know where the time goes.

Steve: You and me, both. I've got a stack of things to do . . . at home, at the office . . . the whole thing gets more overwhelming every day. There's just not enough time to wade through all the stuff.

D: I never realized that raising a child and having a job could be so demanding. And on top of that, my sister wants me to stop by this week and take home a puppy she can't give away.

S: Well, at least you like dogs. I had to mow the damn lawn again this weekend and it took me all day Saturday to do it.

D: So? I had to go to my friend Sue's for lunch . . . that couldn't have been any better. All she ever does is insult me. I don't know why I take it.

S: Sounds like Dave at work. Every time he sees me, he shoves his promotion in my face. I deserved that promotion more than he did! I get so mad thinking about it that is ruins my day.

D: I wouldn't . . .

S: The guy is just lucky and I'm not. There's no other explanation for it.

D: I wouldn't complain . . . you love your work. Mine, on the other hand, well, you know I wanted to be a teacher, not an accountant.

S: But you *chose* accounting.

D: Yes, because I thought I'd make more money and be a CFO by now. Well, I haven't reached my goals and I don't think I ever will! And, in the meantime, I'm stuck doing work I don't enjoy doing.

S: So, why don't we both take a break? Let me take you on a cruise like you've always wanted.

D: That's sweet, Steve . . . but not now. I just can't afford the time. Let's do it next year.

S: That's what you said *last* year.

D: Well, this time I mean it. I just *have* to finish that Anderson audit.

S: I thought you had that all finished weeks ago.

D: Well, basically, I did. But I want to make sure everything is right. I've been going over it to make sure it's perfect.

S: Well, if you can't afford the time for a vacation, at least let's start that exercise regimen the doctor recommended.

D: Who has time for that? I don't think it's worth the effort, anyway. Oh, and in the meantime, will you please call back that guy from the rental agency? He called again today.

S: He did? They're still trying to rip me off for that fifty bucks I was overcharged on the car.

D: You mean that bill *still* isn't settled?

S: Nope . . . and I'll bet I've spent ten hours on the damn thing . . . back and forth between the car rental people and the credit card company. But I'm going to win . . . you can bet on it.

Question 1: What time management mistakes did Diane and/or Steve make? (Use their comments to identify their mistakes.) List your answers in the space provided below.

1.

2.

3.

[Add as many additional answers as you wish]

Question 2: What advice might you give Steve and/or Diane to help them become better time managers? Provide your answers in the space below.

1.

2.

3.

[Add as many additional answers as you wish]

NOTE: A discussion of this exercise (the "right" answers) can be found at the end of this section.

Exercise 1

[To Be Used in Conjunction with Action Step 1 Chapter]

POSSESSION EJECTION CHECKLIST

PURPOSE OF THIS EXERCISE

To identify your major possessions, determine if they are creating more of a hassle than a joy, and take appropriate action.

INSTRUCTIONS

Joyful lives should be "soaring lives"; lives that uplift us and make our spirits rise. Think of yourself in a hot-air balloon, waiting to ascend skyward. You yearn to be free, but your balloon is weighted down with sandbags. The only way to undertake your journey is to jettison the sandbags. Once they are dumped overboard, you can soar from your moorings. That's the way it is with our possessions: When they create more of a hassle than a joy, they bring us down; they are an oppressive weight that compresses our freedom. We need to get rid of these restrictive possessions whenever we can. To help accomplish that objective, I'd like you to make a list of all your *major* possessions in the following space. These should include items like automobiles, boats, significant household goods, even pets—anything that is costing you a significant amount of money and/or time. After you have made your list, think about each item and ask yourself if it has become more of a hassle than a joy. If not, write the word *Keep* to the right of the item. If you're not sure, write the word, *Hold* to the right of the item. If yes, then write the word Jettison to the right of the item. For all those items you decide to jettison, think of the best way to get rid of the item, and then do it! If it is not possible to get rid of the item in your current situation, consider whether you can do so at a future date and, if so, do it then. Remember, the best way to live a joyous, uplifting life is to get rid of the sandbags that are weighing you down . . . even if you have to do it one sandbag at a time.

POSSESSION	KEEP	HOLD	JETTISON
1.			
2.			
3.			
4.			
5.			
6.			
7.			
8.			
9.			
10.			
11.			
12.			
13.			
14.			
15.			
16.			
17.			
18.			
19.			
20.			
21.			
22.			
23.			
24.			
25.			
26.			
27.			
28.			
29.			
30.			

Exercise 2

CASHING IN ON LIFE

PURPOSE OF THIS EXERCISE

To identify those aspects of your life you can enhance by using money and/or trade to purchase positives and sell "shoelaces" in your life.

INSTRUCTIONS

It isn't true—money *can* buy happiness! This happens when we use our financial resources to purchase things that bring us joy and pay others to do things we don't enjoy. Obviously, the amount of discretionary money a person possesses determines, in part, the degree to which financial resources can be expended in the pursuit of a more joyful life. This is a determination each of you must make. However, it is my belief that *each* of us will, at points in our lifetime, have enough discretionary cash or bartering ability to make our lives more joyful. To that end, take some time to list (on the next page) all the things that you don't like to do. Write down *all* the unpleasant tasks you perform . . . tasks you would prefer not to do, if you had the choice. These can involve tasks at home and at work. A good way to remember these tasks is to mentally "run through" your typical daily routines and pinpoint those activities you would rather avoid, be it mowing the lawn or shopping for groceries. Write the tasks in the space provided and then, to the right of each task, indicate if you can afford to pay someone else to do it (write *Pay*) or if you can trade somebody that task for a task you find more enjoyable (write *Barter*). Once you have completed your list, prioritize what tasks are most unpleasant for you and find ways to pay/barter your way out of those first. Go as far down the list as your money/bartering skills allow. Then, do the same with the second list, which asks you to write down all the *positive things* you enjoy—and don't forget to update your list as you encounter new hassles and hopes in your life!

NEGATIVE ITEMS CHECKLIST

TASKS I WOULD PREFER NOT TO DO	IF AFFORDABLE, WRITE "CASH" OR "BARTER"
1.	
2.	
3.	
4.	
5.	
6.	
7.	
8.	
9.	
10.	
11.	
12.	
13.	
14.	
15.	
16.	
17.	
18.	
19.	
20.	
21.	
22.	
23.	
24.	
25.	
26.	
27.	
28.	
29.	
30.	

POSITIVE ITEMS CHECKLIST

THINGS I WANT TO ENJOY/PURCHASE IN LIFE	IF AFFORDABLE, WRITE "CASH" OR "BARTER"
1.	
2.	
3.	
4.	
5.	
6.	
7.	
8.	
9.	
10.	
11.	
12.	
13.	
14.	
15.	
16.	
17.	
18.	
19.	
20.	
21.	
22.	
23.	
24.	
25.	
26.	
27.	
28.	
29.	
30.	

Exercise 3

[To Be Used in Conjunction with Action Step 3 Chapter]

YOU ARE WHO YOU KNOW

PURPOSES OF THIS EXERCISE

To "prune" your interpersonal relationships in a manner that (1) enhances your well-being and self-esteem; and (2) reduces contact with those who exert a *negative influence* on you and limit your ability to live joyfully.

INSTRUCTIONS

We don't always have control over with whom we interact; for example, we might not be able to choose our colleagues at work. However, when we do have a choice in our selection of companions, it is important to choose those individuals who enhance rather than reduce our quality of life. In the space provided, write down the name of every person you interact with on a significant basis (friends, relatives, partners). It doesn't have to be in any order, just make sure you include everyone who is close enough to you to have an impact on the quality of your life. Then, next to the name in the column provided, write down *Positive, Negative,* or *Neutral* based on whether that individual has a *Good, Bad,* or *Indifferent* impact on your life. Take some time to consider your responses, and be honest in your assessments. Then look over your list and see if there is a need to "prune your interpersonal relationships" to grow a healthier network of people around you. It's a critical step in the journey to joyful living.

SIGNIFICANT INDIVIDUALS IN MY LIFE	IMPACT: POSITIVE, NEGATIVE, NEUTRAL
1.	
2.	
3.	
4.	
5.	
6.	
7.	
8.	
9.	
10.	
11.	
12.	
13.	
14.	
15.	
16.	
17.	
18.	
19.	
20.	
21.	
22.	
23.	
24.	
25.	
26.	
27.	
28.	
29.	
30.	

Exercise 4

GET THE GREEN OUT

PURPOSE OF THIS EXERCISE

To identify those individuals who invoke feelings of jealousy in us and make a conscientious effort to overcome the "Green Face Syndrome."

INSTRUCTIONS

Jealousy seems to be an integral part of human nature. Every person I know has experienced it at some point in his or her life; however, that doesn't mean we should accept it as inevitable and unalterable. The truth is jealousy is unhealthy and detrimental to living joyfully; we should strive to reduce this behavior in our own lives whenever possible. To accomplish this objective, take the following steps:

1. Make a list in the space provided of all those individuals toward whom you are jealous.

2. Make a commitment to rid yourself of jealousy toward these individuals. Imagine that each name is on your "Get the Green Out" list, and that each time you can overcome your jealousy toward that person, your list gets smaller.

3. Remind yourself that once you conquer the Green Face Syndrome, you can free up the energy you expended to sustain your jealousy for use in enhancing your own success. The shorter your green list, the quicker that's going to happen!

MY PERSONALIZED "GET THE GREEN OUT" LIST

1.

2.

3.

4.

5.

6.

7.

8.

9.

10.

[If you are jealous of more than ten people, add additional names on the nearest blank page. Also, pay special attention to working on this problem, because you're using a lot of mental energy in a dysfunctional way!]

Exercise 5

[To Be Used in Conjunction with Action Step 5 Chapter]

TEST YOUR LUCK

PURPOSE OF THIS EXERCISE

To remind you of the appropriate way to deal with the luck factor in your life.

INSTRUCTIONS

To paraphrase an old saying, "Luck happens!" All of us experience both bad and good luck in our time on this Earth; what is important is *how we handle luck when it has an impact on our lives.* Based on what you have learned in *Romancing the Clock,* **what *don't* you want to do with your luck . . . and why?** Provide your response in the following box. Then check what you have written against the answer, provided on the next page. Good luck!

THE ANSWER TO THE QUESTION ON LUCK

What you don't want to do with your luck is push it. You push your luck when you let it negatively affect the way you feel about yourself and/or others. You *push it* in the sense that you make it worse through such actions. Any type of luck becomes *unlucky* (and unhealthy) when we let it have a negative impact on the way we feel about ourselves, our time, and/or those around us.

Accentuating the positives and reducing the negatives in your life involves dealing with luck—good or bad—in a healthy and rational manner. It means making the most of good fortune when it comes your way, and getting on with your life when misfortune befalls you.

The next time you experience difficult times in your own life, take heart from the words of a man who turned misfortune (lost his job in a corporate downsizing) into good fortune (in both senses of the word—he founded his own company and made millions!). His insight for us all: I cannot control my luck, but I can control the way I respond to it.

Exercise 6

THE SHADOW KNOWS

PURPOSE OF THIS EXERCISE

To learn more about a specific occupation/profession/job you are interested in pursuing.

INSTRUCTIONS

It amazes me how many individuals take jobs or enter professions with little or no actual knowledge of what will be expected of them—and the kinds of behaviors they will have to undertake—when doing their work. Many of my older students who have quit their jobs and returned to the university tell me "If only I had known what the work was like, I never would have taken the job in the first place."

To help determine if a particular career is right for you, it is important you gain some familiarity with what you would be doing in the workplace if you accepted a specific position. This exercise is designed to help you obtain that information. Here's what you need to do:

1. Decide on a specific job—any job from "A" (Accountant) to "Z" (Zookeeper)—that you might be interested in doing for a living.

2. Call the business of your choice and ask them if you can "shadow" a person who is actually *doing* the job you are interested in pursuing. Most companies and/or self-employed individuals are normally quite willing to grant such a request. *Shadowing* an individual in the workplace involves following them around, watching what it is they do and the tasks they perform. It is called *shadowing* because you remain in the background as an observer—your job is to learn, not participate in the

person's work. You want to remain as unobtrusive as possible, being careful not to create a distraction or impact the work being done. If possible, this shadowing should be conducted during a normal workday (typical for that job) and last the entire day. Hopefully, on completion of your shadowing, you will be able to answer the questions in the next section.

3. If you are not able to shadow a "person of interest," you may be able to get the information you need in a one-on-one interview. Here, you ask the person to describe what he or she does in as much detail as possible. Although not as revealing as shadowing, a good interview can help a prospective employee get a taste of what he or she can expect on the job.

4. Remember, your goal is to gain insight into what a person actually does on the job so you can better determine if that is the kind of work you'll want to do.

After shadowing the person of your choice, answer these questions in the space provided.

1. Describe what the person you shadowed did during his or her workday. Be as specific as possible. (If you are interviewing the person, write down what they said they did.)

2. Based on what you observed during your shadowing assignment (or heard in your interview), do you think you would like to do the kind of work you witnessed or was described to you? Why or why not?

One of the best ways to determine if a job is right for you is to observe a person who has that job and see what the job actually entails. I am always pleased when a reader who has done this exercise tells me, "Once I saw what the job was like, there was no way I wanted anything to do with it." Or, "Having the opportunity to observe a person actually doing the job I wanted convinced me I made the right work choice." The point here is that, although it is not always possible to get a full understanding of what a job is like through one day of workplace observation, it can provide a solid starting point in helping you determine whether a specific career choice is right for you.

Exercise 7

[To Be Used in Conjunction with Action Step 7 Chapter]

GETTING THERE IS [OR SHOULD BE] HALF THE FUN

PURPOSE OF THIS EXERCISE

To realize, recognize, and remember that where we end up on our journey in life is not all that matters. Enjoying the trip along the way is also critical to joyful living.

INSTRUCTIONS

We all aspire to be successful in our undertakings. Wanting to be the best at what we do is both healthy and appropriate. However, it is important to realize that sometimes we cannot reach our goals . . . sometimes we have to be satisfied simply pursuing them.

It is important that whenever you work toward an objective, you find joy in attempting to get there. Thus, it is critical—whenever you set your sights on reaching an objective—that you ask yourself this question: **If I don't actually reach the goal I set out to achieve, will I still enjoy the time spent pursuing my objective?** I recommend you ask this question on a consistent basis whenever you are putting forth significant, long-term effort to reach a goal. When it comes to your occupation, I recommend you revisit this question *at least* once a year. Choose a significant date—like your birthday or New Year's Day—to make your inquiry; this helps you remember to do it on a regular and timely basis. Life is full of destinations. When choosing yours, keep this in mind: If you can revel in the journey, then it's probably a trip worth taking.

Exercise 8

[To Be Used in Conjunction with Action Step 8 Chapter]

TEN THINGS I WANT TO DO BEFORE I DIE

PURPOSES OF THIS EXERCISE

1. To get you thinking about things you want to do in your life.

2. To encourage you to do those things in a timely manner—sooner rather than later—so you can enjoy what is important to you in life while you're still living.

INSTRUCTIONS

It is a sad fact of life, but all of us can probably remember someone who put off doing something they really wanted to do and then ended up dying before they could do it. *Don't be one of those individuals.*

In the following box, list ten things you want to do before you die. It could be a trip. Maybe it's taking a ride in a hot-air balloon or bungee jumping. Perhaps it's deep-sea fishing or bird watching. Let your imagination be your guide . . . dare to dream . . . tap into your "wish list" and don't be shy about it! Even if you currently don't have the financial resources to make a specific wish come true, write it down anyway. Down the road, you might have the funds necessary to get your wish. Also, you don't have to stop at 10 things; that's an arbitrary number. If you can think of 20 things . . . or 50 . . . go ahead and list them all. (And don't be afraid to go back and revisit the list, adding new things as you think about them and crossing out those activities you have already completed.)

Once you have finished your list, make a commitment to begin *doing* the things you have written down. Remember—none of us is immortal, even though we often act as if we were. Don't deprive yourself of the joys you want to experience in life; do them while you still have the chance.

TEN THINGS I WANT TO DO BEFORE I DIE

1.

2.

3.

4.

5.

6.

7.

8.

9.

10.

Exercise 9

[To Be Used in Conjunction with Action Step 9 Chapter]

PERFECTION DETECTION

PURPOSES OF THIS EXERCISE

1. To identify those areas of your life (if any) where you are suffering from the pitfalls of perfectionism.

2. To take steps to reduce "perfectionitis" in those areas, thereby saving time, reducing hassle, and enhancing joyful living.

INSTRUCTIONS

There are very few times when perfection is required to gain the benefits you need from your labors. Yet, it is the difference between performing *competently* and performing *perfectly* that wastes much of our time and robs us of our enjoyment in the things we do. If you suffer from *perfectionitis* in certain (or all) aspects of your life, you will free up time and live more joyfully if you try to overcome this tendency and shoot for doing things well rather than doing things perfectly. To help you achieve this goal,

1. Consider how you conduct yourself in the various areas of your life in the following list.

2. For each area, identify the tasks you perform.

3. Determine if you suffer from perfectionitis in carrying out any (or all) of these tasks.

4. For those tasks you determine you do too perfectly, ask yourself how much you can cut back and still do the tasks well. (You want to aim for a more practical—yet still effective—level of performance.)

5. Make a list of things you can do to achieve competence, not perfection, in these tasks. For example, in doing housework you might decide to wash the sheets and/or dust the house less often than your current once-a-day regimen. Be sure to *write down how you intend to alter your behaviors* and then *put your plan into action.*

6. Finally, if you need some motivation to make these changes in your life, hold on to this thought: How many times have you seen a happy perfectionist?

1. House and yard work (indoor and outdoor cleaning and maintenance).

2. Maintenance and care of your possessions (car, clothes, pets, etc.).

3. Personal grooming.

4. Your work.

5. Your recreation (sports, trips, hobbies, etc.).

6. Your interpersonal relationships (friends, spouse, children).

Exercise 10

DEVELOPING YOUR INDIVIDUAL HEALTH PLAN

PURPOSES OF THIS EXERCISE

1. To encourage you to adopt a healthier lifestyle.

2. To outline the specific things you can do to achieve that healthier lifestyle.

INSTRUCTIONS

Action Step 10 presents several tactics you can use in achieving a healthier and more joyful lifestyle. See if one or more of the following tactics appeal to you. Used individually or in combination, they will improve your life quality . . . and expectancy. Underneath the tactic(s) you are willing to use, write down an "action plan" on how you can incorporate it/them into your daily life. Then, follow your action plan and be prepared to reap the benefits that come with a healthier life.

1. **Reducing excessive stress in your life. (How will you do it?)**

2. The Relaxation Response. (Schedule dates and times.)

3. Exercise. (What type and how often: schedule dates and times.)

4. Reducing "Type-A behavior" in your life. (How will you achieve this objective?)

5. Eating healthfully. (Specify how you will accomplish this objective.)

Exercise 11

[To Be Used in Conjunction with Action Step 11 Chapter]

THE TIME WARRIOR'S CHECKLIST

PURPOSE OF THIS EXERCISE

To remind you how to deal with interpersonal conflict in a manner that minimizes the hassles and time you'll need to spend on this negative activity.

INSTRUCTIONS

Interpersonal conflicts are unavoidable. They are part of living in a society where we must interact with others on a regular basis. However, these conflicts can be reduced in number and severity if—when facing a potential confrontation—you remember to ask yourself the *Time Warrior's* four critical questions and then respond accordingly.

1. **What are my chances of winning this battle?** (Don't fight battles where you have little or no chance of victory.)

2. **Is this battle worth the fight?** (Don't engage in battles where you have to expend more effort than the victory is worth.)

3. **Am I going to win the battle at the cost of losing the war?** (Winning the small victory is not worth losing the big victory.)

4. **Is retreat my best option to secure victory later?** (Sometimes it is best to retreat, regroup, and return when you are in a better position to win the battle.)

   I suggest you actually write these four questions on a card and keep it on top of your desk (or other location where you spend a lot of time) in plain view. That way, when a problem arises, you'll have a ready reminder of what you must ask before determining your course of action. If you get in the habit of using the Time Warrior's four questions on a regular basis when problems occur, you'll find yourself saving a lot of heartache, headache, and hassle. Life will be more joyful, and that, in the final analysis, is what *Romancing the Clock* is all about!

A Discussion of Exercise 1

APPLICATION

(Do not read this material until you have completed Exercise 1)

It is interesting to do Exercise 1 both before and after reading *Romancing the Clock*. If you did it this way, then, hopefully, you can compare the differences between your answers before and after reading the text and get a feeling for what you learned along the way. If, like most readers, you did the exercise **after** reading the book, then the assignment provides you with a useful tool for determining how well you learned—and can apply—the information in *Romancing the Clock*.

The conversation between Diane and Steve was purposely created to highlight each of the 11 time-management errors identified in the book. To check whether you caught the time-management errors, the key word or phrase is highlighted in each sentence of the conversation that relates to one of the 11 time-management mistakes. Then, following the mistake, I list the book chapter ("Action Step") that discusses the highlighted mistake. (You can refer to the designated chapter if you want to discover why the highlighted statement was, in fact, a time-management error.) As you go through the conversation this time, note how often the type of time-management mistakes discussed in this book occur in real life . . . how pervasive they are . . . and how we must remain vigilant if we want to avoid making these errors in our own everyday behaviors.

Steve and Diane's Dialogue with Time Management Errors Identified

(Mistakes are <u>underlined</u>; chapters where mistakes are discussed are in **bold-face** type.)

***

Diane: Last night Gayle called about meeting for lunch. I had to say "no." There's never enough hours in the day. I swear . . . I just don't know where the time goes.

Steve: You and me, both. I've got a stack of things to do . . . at home, at the office . . . the whole thing gets more overwhelming every day. There's just not time enough to wade through all the stuff.

D: I never realized that raising a child and having a job could be so demanding. And on top of that, <u>my sister wants me to stop by this week and take home a puppy</u> she can't give away.

[Action Step 1: Don't accumulate possessions that create more of a hassle than a joy.]

S: Well, at least you like dogs. <u>I had to mow the damn lawn again this weekend and it took me all day Saturday to do it.</u>

[Action Step 2: "Money Is Time": Use it to purchase positives and sell "shoelaces" in your life.]

D: So? I had to go to my friend Sue's for lunch . . . that couldn't have been any better. <u>All she ever does is insult me. I don't know why I take it.</u>

[Action Step 3: Prune your interpersonal relationships.]

S: Sounds like Dave at work. Every time he sees me, he shoves his promotion in my face. <u>I deserved that promotion more than he did! I get so mad thinking about it that it ruins my day.</u>

[Action Step 4: Give the red light to the Green Face Syndrome.]

D: I wouldn't . . .
S: <u>The guy is just lucky and I'm not.</u> There's no other explanation for it.

[Action Step 5: Don't get down on your luck.]

D: I wouldn't complain . . . <u>you love your work. Mine, on the other hand, well, you know I wanted to be a teacher, not an accountant.</u>

[Action Step 6: Choose a career as if a third of your life depended on it. It does.]

S: But you *chose* accounting.
D: <u>Yes, because I thought I'd make more money and be a CFO by now. Well, I haven't reached my goals and I don't think I ever will! And, in the meantime, I'm stuck doing work I don't enjoy.</u>

[Action Step 7: Revel in the journey or skip the trip!]

S: So, why don't we both take a break? Let me take you on a cruise like you've always wanted.

D: <u>That's sweet, Steve. . . but not now. I just can't afford the time. Let's do it next year.</u>

[Action Step 8: Don't always put off until tomorrow that which you can enjoy today.]

S: That's what you said *last* year.

D: Well, this time I mean it. I just *have* to finish that Anderson audit.

S: I thought you had that all finished weeks ago.

D: <u>Well, basically I did. But I want to make sure everything is right. I've been going over it to make sure it's perfect.</u>

[Action Step 9: Avoid the pitfalls of perfectionism.]

S: Well, if you can't afford the time for a vacation . . . at least let's start that exercise regimen the doctor recommended.

D: <u>Who has time for that? I don't think it's worth the effort, anyway.</u>

[Action Step 10: Pursue a healthy lifestyle. It enhances joyful living.]

D: Oh, and in the meantime, will you please call back that guy from the rental agency? He called again today.

S: He did? They're still trying to rip me off for that fifty bucks I was over-charged on the car.

D: You mean that bill *still* isn't settled?

S: <u>Nope . . . and I'll bet I've spent ten hours on the damn thing . . . back and forth between the car rental people and the credit card company. But I'm going to win . . . you can bet on it."</u>

[Action Step 11: When you must do battle . . . pick your fights with care.]

Index

Absenteeism, health-related, 71
Addictive behavior, 10–14
Aerobics, as effective exercise, 77, 79
Aikman, Ann, 79
Alcoholics Anonymous, 89
Appliance repair, 22
Attitudes
   negative, 25–27, 42, 98–101
   passive, 76
   positive, 41, 42, 98–101
   toward excessive stress, 73–74
   toward luck, 40–41
   toward work, 2

Balance, 64
Bartering, 18, 51
Benson, Herbert, 74–77
Biological clock, 65
Black, Alice and Bill, 8–10
Boredom, 51–55

Capitalism, 5, 20
Car repair, 22
Career. *See* Worklife
Choices
   between careers and parenthood, 64–65
   in buying quality time, 17–18
   in worklife, 46, 50
   of interpersonal relationships, 28
Common sense/common practice, 4
Comparison shopping, 22
Competence, *vs.* perfection, 67–69
Competitiveness
   and Type A behavior, 81
   for rewards and benefits, 20, 32
Compulsive striving, 80
Conflicts. *See* Interpersonal conflicts
Conrad, C. Carson, 77
Conspicuous consumption, 5
Control
   luck and, 40–42, 41
   of interpersonal conflicts, 87
   of stress, 74–85

   of your own destiny, 59
   over interpersonal relationships, 28
Cooper, Ken, 78, 80
Cost/benefit analyses, 9
Custer, George, General, 95, 97

Delivery services, 21
Dylan, Bob, 31, 33–34

Ego, retreat and, 96
Elitism, 20
Energy, saving, 32, 34
Excess, 10, 73–74
Exercise
   safety precautions and, 79–80
   stress and, 77–79

Fable of the dog and the bone, 33
Fame, 34
Fight or flight response, 72–73
Fink, David, 55–56
Frequent flyer mileage, 22
Friedman, Meyer, 80–84

Gamblers
   addiction and, 11–14
   retreating and, 96
Gilmore, C.P., 77–78
Goals
   achievement of, 59–60
   career, 46
   satisfaction in pursuing, 57–61
Goleman, Daniel, 77
Gradual decay function, in job performance, 53
Green Face Syndrome, 29–34, 36

Health. *See* Stress
Household tasks, paying others to do, 21
Hump night, 45
"Humpty-Dumpty" moment, 27–28
Hurry sickness, 80

Immortality, 34
Impulse purchases, 9

Inertia, retreat and, 96
Internet, for services, 22
Interpersonal conflicts
  fighting losing battles, 88–89
  fighting worthless battles, 89–92
  retreat and, 95–97
  winning battles but losing the war, 92–95
Interpersonal relationships
  and the "Humpty-Dumpty" moment, 27–28
  pruning, 27–28
  unhealthy, 25–27

Jealousy, 29–34
Job. *See* Worklife
Job enrichment, 53–54
Johnson, Wendy, 71–72

Klipper, Miriam, 74–77
Knowles, John, 72

Latchkey children, 65
Luck, 35–42

MacArthur, Douglas, General, 97
Marriage
  and changing one's spouse, 88–89
  boredom in, 55
  careers and parenthood and, 64–65
McQuade, Walter, 79
Meditation, 75
Miracle Man, 25–26
Moderation, 10, 85
Money, and time, 15–23

Negativism, of other people, 25–27

OCD (obsessive-compulsive disorder), perfectionism and, 68

Parenthood, careers and, 64–65
Perfectionism
  and OCD (obsessive-compulsive disorder), 68
  competence *vs.,* 67–69
Perseverance, 95
Pessimists, 40–41
Planning, 46, 65
Polyphasic, 82
Possessions
  accumulation of, 5
  as a burden, 6–7
  becoming addictions, 10–14
  how to hassle-proof, 8–9
Premiums, paying for services, 22
President's Council on Physical Fitness, 77
Profession. *See* Worklife

Quality time, 2
  bartering for, 18
  buying, 15–17
  guidelines for buying, 19
  jealousy and, 31
  worklife and, 45
Quantity time, 2

Relaxation response, stress and, 74–77
Restaurants, 22
Retraining, 46
Retreating, 95–97
Rogers, Kenny, 96
Rosenman, Ray, 80–84
Running, as effective exercise, 78

Self-fulfilling prophecy, 26
Selfless/selfish behavior, 64
Selye, Hans, 45–46, 73
Serenity Prayer, 89
SNIOP (Susceptible to the Negative Influence of Other People), 26
Sports, as effective exercise, 77
Star Trek—the Prime Directive, 100
Stress
  and effective exercise, 77–80
  and the culmination of small annoyances, 21
  and the relaxation response, 74–77
  and Type A behavior, 80–85
  attitudes toward, 73–74
  definition of, 72–73
  diseases related to, 73
  medical dangers of, 55, 71–72, 84
  moderation and, 85
  possessions and, 14
  worklife and, 45–46
Success, in reaching goals, 60

Taxis, 22
Telephone service, 22
Thoreau, Henry David, 3
Ticket agencies, using, 21
Time management, 2–3
Tipping, 22
Twain, Mark, 36
Type A Behavior and Your Heart, 81, 84
Type A personality
  self-identification test for, 81–83
  stress and, 80–85
Type B personality, 81, 83

Valet parking, 22
Value systems, 17

Walking, as effective exercise, 78
Warranties, 22
Wealth, accumulation of, 5
Worklife
  and Aspiration-Occupation (A-O) Exercise, 46–49
  and seeking new employment, 55–56
  boredom and, 51–55
  enjoyment of, 45–46
  increasing satisfaction of, 46–49, 50–51
  length of, 45
  options for, 50
  stress and, 45–46

Zera, Sue, 35–36